REAL LIFE
RECIPES

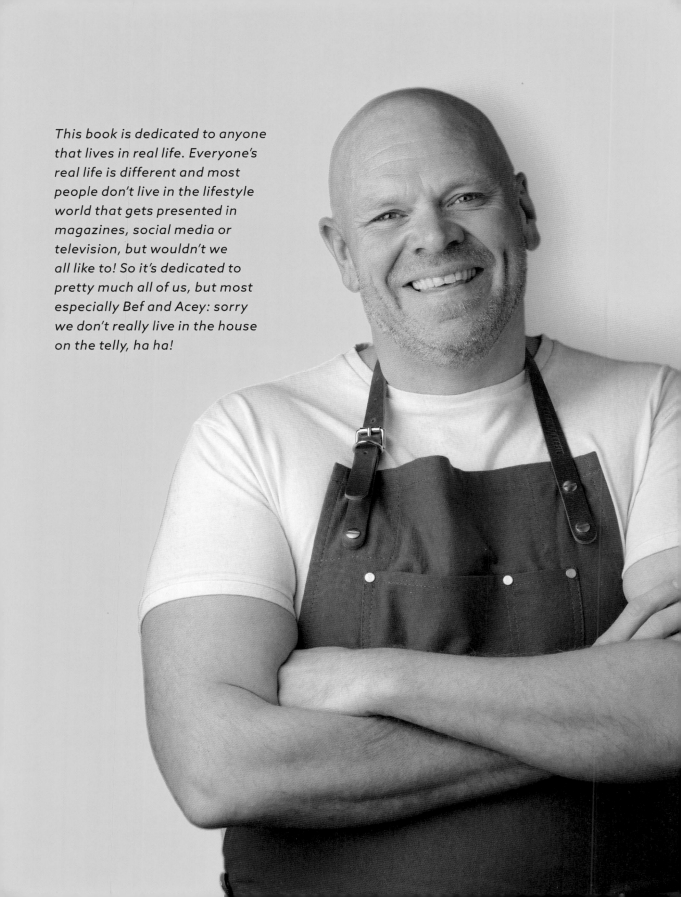

This book is dedicated to anyone that lives in real life. Everyone's real life is different and most people don't live in the lifestyle world that gets presented in magazines, social media or television, but wouldn't we all like to! So it's dedicated to pretty much all of us, but most especially Bef and Acey: sorry we don't really live in the house on the telly, ha ha!

TOM KERRIDGE
REAL LIFE
RECIPES

FANTASTIC FUSS-FREE FOOD

BLOOMSBURY ABSOLUTE

LONDON · OXFORD · NEW YORK · NEW DELHI · SYDNEY

10
LUNCH

Flexible ideas for creating something quick and tasty, because
a proper lunch is the reset button for the rest of your day.

70
TEA

Dinnertime recipes to make you feel good when life gets busy,
and answer the eternal question: what's for tea?

150

SOMETHING A BIT
FANCIER

Dishes that are all about remembering how to enjoy the process
of cooking again. Put in a bit of effort to show you care!

206

TREATS

Making treats is creative and good fun – and the end result always
tastes so much better than anything you can buy.

KEEPING IT REAL

I want this to be the book you look to for inspiration, for meals that feel realistic and fit in with your life. We all have a lot going on these days, juggling work and family with seeing friends and making time for all the things we enjoy. Because of this, it can be easy to get into the routine of cooking the same few dishes each week, while on social media it seems as though other people are entertaining friends with three-course dinners on a Tuesday night! I know that real life tends to be messier and more spontaneous than that, and I want the recipes in this book to reflect the reality of our lives today. I hope to show you that however much time you have, cooking is a chance to get creative in the kitchen and to do something special for the people you care about.

As a business owner and chef, it often feels like I'm rushing from meeting to meeting to phone call to home and back again – and I think many people can relate to that feeling. It also means I'm not always around to eat tea with my son Acey, so when I am at home in the week or at weekends, I make it a priority to do some cooking with him (a cheesy omelette or easy pasta dish, or we might make a cake). Not eating as a family every night is a common scenario for lots of working parents with young children – we need to be honest about this and recognise

that there's nothing wrong with it. All it means is that it's up to us to make the times we *are* around count. Like most children, Acey will go through phases of absolutely loving eating something and then change his mind and say he doesn't like it halfway through cooking it. And I have the same problem as every other parent; it doesn't matter who their dad is – getting kids to eat vegetables is a nightmare! So, we cook things that will engage him and help him understand where food comes from.

On a Sunday, I often do a big roast or slow-cooked stew, and that's when we all get together and spend some proper time as a family or with friends. I love planting the seed in people's minds by saying, 'Right, tomorrow we're having beef stew,' and getting everyone excited about what we're going to be eating. There's nothing better than filling the house with the delicious smells of whatever it is you're cooking. At the same time, please don't put any pressure on yourself to try to live a picture-perfect lifestyle if that's not your reality. Trust me, it's few people's reality! And I really don't care if you have a bottle of brown sauce or ketchup on the table at teatime either. I'll let you into a secret you might not see on my own social media: I often can't resist a good dollop of brown sauce too!

Although I would love it if we could all spend an hour or two wandering around a fruit and veg market each day, and visit the butcher's or fishmonger's, most people tend to do a big supermarket shop once a week to stock up on the basics – chicken, fish, mince, a bit of fruit and veg, a few tins for the cupboard, pasta and rice, some extras for the freezer.

I completely understand the ease of doing an online shop in your lunch break to arrive at 9pm the next day. I really don't think convenience should be seen as a bad word. It's about streamlining, systemising and making your life more efficient. We all want to be happier and healthier, and if doing an online shop can help you get a better work-life balance then I'm all for it.

Through quick ways to add maximum flavour and clever hacks in the kitchen, I want to share with you how to make the most of your supermarket staples.

The four chapters in this book reflect how I think most of us really cook. In the **Lunch** chapter, for example, there are ideas for quick, tasty meals you can rustle up in between video calls if you find yourself working from home. Many of these can also be scaled up for the weekend if you are feeding a crowd, or packed up for later if you're heading out to the office.

The biggest chapter is **Tea** because I know that this is what most people find the trickiest. These recipes mostly use basic ingredients from your regular weekly shop, with a few extras you can pick up on the way home or add to your shopping list next time, to give your dinner a fresh spin and make it feel a bit more special. And because time is sometimes tight, lots of these recipes can be served up in half an hour.

At the weekend or if you have friends coming round on a week night, you might be in the mood for **Something a Bit Fancier**, and these are the recipes to take your time over. Some of them take more time to prep, but there's nothing complicated about them and they all use ingredients that you know and can find easily. Play around with some new techniques, maybe get other people involved. It's a chance to stop rushing around and really get back into enjoying the cooking process.

The final chapter is **Treats** – the cakes, cookies, puddings and desserts. Making and eating these is all about having some fun. You might not have time to bake sweet things on a normal weekday, but most of mine can be made when it suits you and then enjoyed over the next few days.

I've also included a bit of handy signposting on the recipes, so it's easy to find these specific ones if you want to:

QUICK — Ready on the table in around 30 minutes.

LOW SHOP — Uses mostly basics or store-cupboard ingredients, with a few extra bits and bobs from the shop.

MAKE AHEAD — Suitable for freezing, or keeping in the fridge to serve up later.

COOKS ITSELF — Once the prepping's done, leave to cook while you get on with other things.

On pages 36–7 you'll find my list of Flavour Boosts – the big bold ingredients I use to add instant nuggets of flavour when I'm cooking. You can read about some brilliant timesaving cheat's ingredients on pages 102–3, because even as a professional chef I'm happy to use packets and jars of ready-made stuff if that speeds things up at home. And don't worry if you're missing a couple of ingredients for a recipe: on pages 164–5 I've provided a guide to easy swaps so you can make the best use of what you already have. There's also a list of the kit that I find most useful on pages 234–5.

Most of all, I'd like this book to enable us all to eat tasty, satisfying meals in a way that reflects how we're cooking today. These recipes aren't just about the speedy lunches and teas that can come from a supermarket trolley, they're also about remembering how to enjoy cooking and have some fun with it.

I'd love it if you were to have a quick look through the pages and think, 'Brilliant, let's do that tomorrow – I'll pick up some herbs or feta or a packet of ready-rolled pastry on the way home.' I know most of us are balancing work and home life and it can be really hard at times. I get it, I really do. I hope these recipes mean there's one less thing on your list to stress about. Just get stuck in and enjoy the chaos!

LUNCH

TOMATO BURRATA SALAD

Creamy burrata, roasted and fresh tomatoes, crunchy baguette
toasts and lightly pickled shallots give a bit of an upgrade
to a dish we all know and love. Using fresh pesto from a tub
provides a more vibrant flavour, but jarred pesto is a great
store-cupboard alternative.

SERVES 2

12 thin slices olive baguette

1 tbsp extra virgin olive oil

2 bunches cherry tomatoes
on-the-vine

Salt and freshly ground
black pepper

PICKLED SHALLOT

1 banana shallot, finely
sliced into rings

2 tbsp red wine vinegar

2 tsp caster sugar

SALAD DRESSING

2 tbsp extra virgin olive oil

1 tbsp pesto

1 tsp white wine vinegar

FRESH TOMATOES

2 large ripe Iberico
tomatoes, cut into wedges

80g mixed cherry
tomatoes, halved

TO ASSEMBLE

2 burrata (100g each)

A small handful of basil
leaves

2 tbsp pine nuts, toasted

1. Preheat the oven to 200°C/Fan 180°C/Gas 6. Line 2 small
baking trays with baking paper.

2. Brush the baguette slices with the extra virgin olive oil,
sprinkle with a little salt and lay them on one of the baking
trays. Place on a high shelf in the oven for 10–12 minutes
or until light golden and crispy.

3. Lay the bunches of cherry tomatoes on the other lined
tray. Sprinkle with salt and pepper and place in the oven for
around 8 minutes until they just begin to burst. Remove and
leave to cool.

4. For the pickled shallot, put the shallot rings into a small
heatproof bowl and add the wine vinegar and sugar. Pour on
just enough boiling water to cover the shallot and stir well.
Set aside to cool and pickle lightly.

5. Mix the salad dressing ingredients together in a large bowl
and season with salt and pepper. Add the large tomatoes
and cherry tomatoes and mix well.

6. Arrange the dressed fresh tomatoes on serving plates
and add the toasted baguette slices. Place a vine of roasted
cherry tomatoes and a burrata on each plate and pour over
any remaining dressing and juices from the tomato tray.

7. Scatter the pickled shallot rings and basil leaves over the
salad and sprinkle with the toasted pine nuts to serve.

PEA SOUP WITH CRISPY HAM CROÛTONS

Gnarly chunks of sourdough and crispy Parma ham take regular croûtons up a notch in this easy pea and pancetta soup. You won't believe how speedy and delicious it is to make – using a bag of frozen peas.

SERVES 4

50g butter

150g pancetta, diced

3 banana shallots, finely diced

2 garlic cloves, sliced

700ml chicken stock

2 tbsp mint leaves, roughly chopped

200ml single cream

800g frozen peas

Salt and freshly ground black pepper

CRISPY HAM CROÛTONS

2 thick slices sourdough

2 tbsp extra virgin olive oil

1 garlic clove, finely grated

1 tbsp flat-leaf parsley, finely chopped

6 slices Parma ham

TO FINISH

Pea shoots or watercress

1. First, prepare the croûtons. Preheat the oven to 200°C/ Fan 180°C/Gas 6. Tear the sourdough into bite-sized pieces and toss with the olive oil, garlic and parsley on a small baking tray. Sprinkle with salt and pepper and mix well with your hands until the bread is coated evenly. Spread out on the tray.

2. Place the tray on a high shelf in the oven for 8 minutes. Tear the Parma ham slices in half. Take the baking tray from the oven and lay the Parma ham over the croûtons. Return to the oven for 8–10 minutes or until the croûtons are deep golden and the Parma ham is crispy, then remove and set aside until needed.

3. While the croûtons are in the oven, make the soup. Melt the butter in a saucepan over a high heat. Once melted and foaming, add the pancetta and stir over the heat for about 5 minutes until it begins to caramelise. Add the shallots and garlic to the pan and sauté for 2–3 minutes or until softened.

4. Stir in the chicken stock, chopped mint and cream and bring the soup to a low simmer. Let it simmer gently for 3 minutes and then add the frozen peas. Stir and bring back to a simmer then remove the pan from the heat.

5. Blitz the soup until smooth, using a stick blender or jug blender, and season with salt and pepper to taste. Divide between warmed bowls and top each portion with crispy ham croûtons and pea shoots or watercress to serve.

FISH FRITTERS WITH SOURED CREAM DIP

You can use any fish you like for these fritters, which are cooked like drop scones. Cod, haddock, hake and salmon all work well.

MAKES 20–24

300g skinless firm white fish or salmon fillet

300g smooth mashed potato (leftover or freshly cooked)

½ tsp sweet smoked paprika

2 tbsp baby capers

2 tbsp dill leaves, chopped

2 tbsp flat-leaf parsley, finely chopped

Finely grated zest of 1 lemon

6 tbsp plain flour

150ml natural yoghurt

2 free-range eggs, separated

Mild olive oil, to cook

Salt and freshly ground black pepper

SOURED CREAM DIP

50ml mayonnaise

100ml soured cream

Juice of 1 lemon

1 tsp mild mustard

½ tsp smoked paprika

1 tbsp dill leaves, finely chopped

1. Preheat the oven to 150°C/Fan 130°C/Gas 2.

2. Cut the fish fillet into 1cm dice. Place in a bowl with the mashed potato, paprika, capers, dill, parsley and lemon zest and mix well. Add the flour, yoghurt, egg yolks and some salt and pepper and give it another mix to combine.

3. In a clean bowl, whisk the egg whites until they form stiff peaks. Add half of the whisked whites to the fish mixture in the bowl and stir well to incorporate. Add the rest of the whisked whites and fold in gently, using a spatula or large metal spoon – to create a light batter.

4. For the dip, mix all the ingredients together in a small bowl and season with salt and pepper to taste. Set aside until needed.

5. You will need to cook the fish fritters in 2 or 3 batches. Place a large non-stick frying pan over a medium-high heat and add 2 tbsp olive oil. When the pan is hot, drop in heaped tablespoonfuls of the fritter mixture, spacing them apart.

TO SERVE

Lemon wedges

Mixed leaf salad

Leave to cook for 2 minutes or so, then flip each one over and cook for 2–3 minutes on the other side.

6. As the fritters are cooked, transfer them to a baking tray and keep warm in the low oven, while you cook the rest, adding a little more oil to the pan if needed.

7. Once the fish fritters are all cooked, serve them with the soured cream dip, lemon wedges and a salad on the side.

OPEN CROQUE MONSIEUR

This is next-level cheese on toast! Layers of thick and creamy béchamel, two types of cheese, a little heat from the mustard and sliced ham in the middle. What more could you want? It takes longer to put together than regular cheese on toast but I guarantee it's worth the effort.

MAKES 2

30g butter

20g plain flour

250ml whole milk

2 thick slices sourdough

2 tsp Dijon or English mustard

60g Comté or Cheddar, grated

60g Gruyère, grated

150g thick sliced ham

Salt and freshly ground black pepper

TO SERVE

Mixed leaf salad

Cornichons

1. Melt the butter in a small saucepan over a medium heat, then add the flour and cook, stirring gently, for 1 minute. Gradually add the milk, whisking well after each addition. Keep whisking gently over the heat for 3–4 minutes or until the béchamel sauce is simmering and thickened. Season with salt and pepper to taste.

2. Transfer the béchamel to a bowl, cover the surface with a piece of baking paper to prevent a skin forming and place in the fridge to cool down.

3. Preheat the oven to 220°C/Fan 200°C/Gas 7. Line a baking tray with baking paper.

4. Toast the sourdough slices and spread with your favourite mustard on one side. Mix the grated cheeses together. When the béchamel is cool, spoon a layer on top of the mustard and add a sprinkling of cheese. Add a layer of ham and then spread with the rest of the béchamel and sprinkle on a final layer of grated cheese.

5. Pop the cheese and ham toasts on the lined baking tray and place on the top shelf of the oven. Cook for around 8 minutes until the cheese is golden and bubbling on top. If you want some more colour on the cheese, place under the grill for the final 1–2 minutes.

6. Serve the croque monsieur with a mixed leaf salad alongside and some cornichons to cut through the richness.

ASPARAGUS & COURGETTE SALAD

Asparagus isn't in season for long, so this is a way to make a bit of a song and dance about it when it's around. A low-effort salad and a play on a classic salade niçoise, it's also good for using up any leftover bread.

SERVES 2

6 baby courgettes, halved lengthways

12 asparagus spears, trimmed

1 small garlic clove, finely grated

Finely grated zest of ½ lemon

2 tbsp extra virgin olive oil

½ stale baguette, thinly sliced

2 large free-range eggs

6 cooked new potatoes

6 radishes, finely sliced

12 Nocellara green olives

Salt and freshly ground black pepper

DRESSING

1 tsp Dijon mustard

2 tsp sherry vinegar

3 tbsp extra virgin olive oil

½ tsp honey

TO FINISH

Parmesan shavings

1. Preheat the oven to 200°C/Fan 180°C/Gas 6.

2. Put the courgettes, asparagus, garlic and lemon zest in a shallow dish. Add half the olive oil, season with salt and pepper and mix well. Set aside to marinate.

3. Lay the baguette slices on a baking tray and brush with the remaining olive oil. Place on a high shelf in the oven for around 8–10 minutes until lightly toasted.

4. Bring a medium saucepan of water to the boil, add the eggs and cook for 6 minutes (to soft-cook the yolks; the whites will be firm). Lift out the eggs, cool under running water, then peel and halve lengthways. Cut the cooked potatoes in half, too.

5. Place a large non-stick frying pan over a high heat. Add the marinated courgette halves, cut side down, and sauté for 2–3 minutes, turning them over once. Remove from the pan.

6. Add the asparagus spears to the pan, together with any leftover marinade. Cook for 1 minute, adding a splash of water to the pan, to help them steam-cook. Remove the pan from the heat.

7. Divide the courgettes, asparagus, new potatoes, boiled eggs, radishes and olives between serving plates and add the toasted baguette slices.

8. Whisk the dressing ingredients together in a small bowl to combine and spoon liberally over each salad. Scatter over some Parmesan shavings and tuck in!

HAM & CHEESE OMELETTE

Omelette-making is an excellent life skill to have – just make sure you use a good non-stick pan. This is a real go-to dish in our house and it's one that Acey likes to cook with me. Use your favourite cheese – or whatever you have in the fridge – and experiment with different fillings.

SERVES 1

2 large free-range eggs

2 tbsp single cream

1 tsp finely chopped chives

A small knob of butter

50g thick sliced ham, diced

25g Cheddar, grated

Salt and freshly ground pepper

1. Put the eggs, cream and chopped chives into a small bowl and season with salt and pepper. Beat well with a fork or a small whisk until well combined.

2. Put a 20cm non-stick frying pan over a medium-high heat. Add the butter to the pan and when it's melted and foaming, pour in the beaten eggs. Leave them for a few seconds, then when they start to set around the edges, agitate them gently with a rubber spatula and reduce the heat.

3. Scatter the ham over one side of the omelette and the cheese over the other. When the egg looks half cooked, loosen the edges with the spatula and fold the omelette over in half. Let it cook for 30 seconds and then flip it over and leave to cook on the other side for 30 seconds.

4. Remove from the heat and slide the omelette onto a warm plate. Serve with hot buttered toast and a side salad for a more substantial lunch.

HALLOUMI, GREEN BEAN & RED PEPPER SALAD

Torn-up pitta bread acts like croûtons and provides a satisfying garlicky crunch in this Greek-style salad. Sweet honey in the dressing combines beautifully with the salty pan-fried halloumi, olives and smoky roasted red peppers.

SERVES 2

2 pitta breads

2 tbsp extra virgin olive oil

2 tbsp oregano leaves, finely chopped

1 garlic clove, finely grated

200g green beans, blanched

100g roasted red peppers (from a jar), thickly sliced

250g block halloumi, cut into 6 slices

A large handful of mixed salad leaves

A handful of Kalamata olives

Salt and freshly ground black pepper

DRESSING

3 tbsp extra virgin olive oil

1 tbsp sherry vinegar

2 tsp honey

1. Preheat the oven to 200°C/Fan 180°C/Gas 6.

2. Tear the pitta breads into bite-sized pieces and place on a baking tray. Drizzle over 1 tbsp extra virgin olive oil and sprinkle with half the oregano. Add the garlic and season liberally with salt and pepper. Mix together with your hands, making sure you rub all the garlic and olive oil into the pitta.

3. Put the tray on a high shelf in the oven for 8–10 minutes or until the pitta is golden and crispy. Remove and set aside until needed.

4. For the dressing, in a large bowl, mix the extra virgin olive oil, sherry vinegar and honey together and season with a little salt and pepper.

5. Add the green beans and roasted peppers to the dressing and toss to combine.

6. Put a small non-stick frying over a medium heat. Sprinkle the halloumi slices on both sides with the remaining oregano and a little salt and pepper. When the pan is hot, add the remaining 1 tbsp olive oil and place the halloumi slices in the pan. Cook for 2 minutes on each side or until golden brown.

7. Add half the toasted pitta to the bowl of green beans and roasted peppers, along with the salad leaves and olives. Toss to mix and divide the salad between two plates. Top with the cooked halloumi and remaining pitta croûtons to serve.

CHARGRILLED CHICKEN & NOODLE SALAD

Every mouthful of this chicken noodle salad has something extra going on – fresh crunch from the cucumber, mangetout and carrot, fiery heat from the chilli, citrus from the dressing and bright freshness from the lemongrass – all finished off with roasted peanuts and juicy lime.

SERVES 2

2 skinless, boneless chicken breasts

2 tsp lemongrass paste

1 tbsp soy sauce

120g vermicelli rice noodles

1 large carrot, julienned

½ cucumber, julienned

12 mangetout, halved on an angle

1 tbsp vegetable oil

DRESSING

Juice of 2 limes

1 tbsp soy sauce

2 tsp sugar

TO FINISH & SERVE

1 green chilli, finely sliced

2 tbsp roasted peanuts, roughly chopped

Coriander

Lime wedges

1. Take each chicken breast and bash it gently with a rolling pin to flatten it out to an even thickness (this will help it to cook evenly). Mix the lemongrass paste and soy sauce together in a shallow dish, add the chicken and turn to coat, then set aside to marinate.

2. Put the noodles into a heatproof bowl and pour on enough boiling water to cover them. Leave to soften for 10 minutes.

3. Meanwhile, mix the ingredients together for the dressing.

4. When the noodles are softened, drain and run cold water over them to cool. Drain again and place in a bowl with the carrot, cucumber and mangetout. Add the dressing and toss to mix well.

5. Place a chargrill pan over a medium-high heat. Drizzle the oil over the chicken fillets and lay them in the pan. Cook for 2–3 minutes on each side. Remove to a warm plate and leave to rest for a minute.

6. Divide the noodle salad between serving bowls. Slice the chicken and place on top of the noodles. Sprinkle with some chilli slices, chopped peanuts and coriander and serve, with lime wedges on the side.

BEETROOT & GOAT'S CHEESE GALETTE

Deceptively easy to make, this galette looks really special in the middle of the table. Beetroot and goat's cheese are a classic pairing, while caramelised onion chutney brings sweetness, the ricotta provides a lovely dairy acidity and hazelnuts add a satisfying crunch. *Pictured overleaf*

SERVES 4-6

500g pack ready-made shortcrust pastry

Plain flour, to dust

250g ricotta

Finely grated zest of ½ lemon

2 tbsp thyme leaves

3 tbsp caramelised onion chutney

500g cooked beetroot, sliced

150g goat's cheese log, thinly sliced

40g hazelnuts, halved

1 large free-range egg, beaten with a pinch of salt, to glaze

Salt and freshly ground black pepper

Extra virgin olive oil, to finish

Mixed leaf salad, to serve

1. Preheat the oven to 200°C/Fan 180°C/Gas 6 and place a large baking tray inside to heat up.

2. Lay a large piece of baking paper on your work surface and dust with a little flour. Place the pastry on the paper and roll it out to a 34cm circle. Leaving a 3cm margin around the edge (this will form a rim), prick the pastry well with a fork.

3. Mix the ricotta with the lemon zest and half the thyme leaves and season with a little salt and pepper.

4. Spread the onion chutney over the pastry base and then spoon on the ricotta mixture, spreading it in an even layer.

5. Distribute the beetroot slices evenly over the ricotta, overlapping them slightly, and season with a little salt and pepper. Arrange the goat's cheese slices on top of the beetroot and scatter the hazelnuts evenly over the top.

6. Brush the pastry margin with beaten egg. Sprinkle over the remaining thyme leaves and then start to fold the pastry margin up over the edge of the filling, pressing each fold firmly until all the edges are folded inwards to form a rim. Brush the top of the folded pastry edges liberally with the remaining beaten egg.

7. Slide a flat baking tray under the baking paper and galette. Take the hot tray from the oven and carefully slide the galette off its tray and onto the hot tray.

8. Place the galette on a high shelf in the oven and cook for 35–40 minutes or until the pastry is a deep golden brown.

9. Remove the galette from the oven and leave it to sit for a few minutes. Drizzle a little extra virgin olive oil over the surface and cut the galette into thick wedges. Serve with a leafy salad on the side.

SMOKED SALMON PATTIES, BEETROOT & APPLE SALAD

Who doesn't love a super-posh fish cake? These use fresh salmon to keep everything nice and moist, and smoked salmon for a real punch of flavour, along with capers and dill. The salad brings a sharp acidity that cuts through any richness.

SERVES 4

2 tbsp olive oil

2 banana shallots, diced

2 garlic cloves, finely chopped

500g fresh salmon fillet

100g smoked salmon

1 large free-range egg

2 tbsp baby capers

Finely grated zest of 1 lemon

2 tsp Dijon mustard

2 tbsp dill leaves, chopped

50g fresh breadcrumbs

Salt and freshly ground black pepper

Lemon wedges, to serve

SALAD

2 cooked beetroot

2 Granny Smiths (or other crisp, tart eating apples)

1 tbsp crème fraîche

1 tbsp extra virgin olive oil

Juice of 1 lemon

1 tsp honey

1 tsp wholegrain mustard

50g watercress

1. Heat 1 tbsp of the olive oil in a medium frying pan over a medium-high heat. Add the shallots and garlic and sauté for 2–3 minutes or until tender. Remove from the heat and leave to cool.

2. Cut the fresh salmon fillet in half. Cut one half into large chunks and place in a food processor, along with the smoked salmon and egg. Pulse until you have a smooth paste. Scrape the mixture into a large bowl.

3. Dice the remaining fresh salmon and add it to the bowl along with the capers, lemon zest, mustard, chopped dill and breadcrumbs. Season with salt and pepper and mix well.

4. Form this mixture into 4 large patties, or 8 smaller ones. Place on a tray in the fridge to firm up for 15 minutes. (If you are making the patties ahead, cover and keep in the fridge until ready to cook.)

5. For the salad, cut the beetroot and apples into julienne and place in a bowl. Add all the other ingredients, except the watercress, and toss to combine.

6. Place the frying pan over a medium-high heat and add the remaining 1 tbsp olive oil. When it is hot, add the patties to the pan. Cook big patties for 3–4 minutes on each side; allow 2–3 minutes on each side for the smaller ones.

7. Add the watercress to the beetroot and apple salad and divide between serving plates. Add the hot salmon patties to the plates and serve, with lemon wedges.

HARISSA-ROAST PUMPKIN & FETA SALAD

Roasting pumpkin or butternut squash brings out all its natural sugars, which is perfect next to the spicy kick from rose harissa and contrasting cooling feta cheese. The roasted chickpeas and toasted pumpkin seeds provide a delicious, moreish crunch.

SERVES 2

500g deseeded pumpkin (or butternut squash), cut into wedges

400g tin chickpeas, rinsed and drained

4 tbsp extra virgin olive oil

1 tbsp rose harissa

1 tsp wholegrain mustard

Juice of ½ lemon

1 tbsp white balsamic vinegar

100g baby spinach leaves

100g feta

Salt and freshly ground black pepper

2 tbsp pumpkin seeds, toasted, to finish

1. Preheat the oven to 200°C/Fan 180°C/Gas 6.

2. Place the pumpkin (or squash) and chickpeas on a baking tray. Drizzle with 1 tbsp of the extra virgin olive oil and the harissa and sprinkle with salt and pepper. Mix well with your hands so that both the pumpkin and chickpeas are coated well. Roast on a high shelf in the oven for 20–25 minutes, or until just tender.

3. Meanwhile, for the dressing, in a medium bowl, mix together the mustard, lemon juice, balsamic vinegar and remaining 3 tbsp olive oil. Season with salt and pepper to taste. Transfer 2 tbsp of the dressing to a small bowl and set aside.

4. Take the tray of pumpkin (or squash) and chickpeas from the oven and set aside to cool slightly.

5. Add the spinach leaves to the dressing in the medium bowl and toss gently to coat. Divide the spinach between two plates.

6. Distribute the roasted pumpkin (or squash) wedges and chickpeas over the spinach and crumble over the feta. Sprinkle with the toasted pumpkin seeds and trickle over the reserved dressing to serve.

FLAVOUR BOOSTS

With one or two high-flavour, big-impact ingredients you can short-cut your way to more delicious mealtimes without having to spend ages in the kitchen. Some of these may sound a bit luxurious, but you only need small amounts to create intense nuggets of flavour.

CHEESE When it comes to adding extra oomph to meals, it's hard to beat cheese. Good melty ones include mozzarella, Gruyère, Monterey Jack and Comté. A strong Cheddar is a great all-rounder, and I love the tangy intensity of blue cheeses. I also use ricotta for its smooth acidity, feta for salty freshness, slightly chewy (and satisfyingly squeaky) pan-fried halloumi, creamy goat's cheese and sharp Parmesan. Even just a few shavings of cheese on top of your pasta, soup or salad will add a whole new layer of flavour.

CHILLIES Fresh chillies, dried chilli flakes and chilli powder add warmth and depth to stir-fries, curries, salads and pasta dishes. Chillies and chilli powder come in different strengths, so work out what your preferences are, and remember a little goes a long way.

CURED HAM Parma ham, bacon lardons and pancetta bring an intense smokiness to all kinds of dishes, from bolognese to traybakes, stews and pies. Pepperoni and chorizo will also add a subtle peppery heat.

DAIRY A splash of cream adds a touch of luxury to soups, sauces, dressings, curries, tarts and mashed potato. I also like crème fraîche for its sharp acidity and freshness – stir it through mash for a lighter taste and creamy texture.

FLAVOUR ENHANCERS Salty and umami, a spoonful of those store-cupboard classics, Marmite, Bovril or Worcestershire sauce, will help bring out the flavours in your cooking, especially in meaty dishes. Porcini mushroom paste has a fantastic umami flavour and works in a similar way; it is available from most big supermarkets.

GINGER, LEMONS AND LIMES These all add an instant lift and freshness to sweet and savoury dishes. They're ideal for quick salad dressings too.

HERBS Fresh herbs add flavour, texture and colour. Tarragon and chicken are a beautiful pairing, dill goes well with fish, and mint and basil are great in salads. Flat-leaf parsley, chives, coriander, thyme and rosemary are all pretty versatile. Dried herbs are a good store-cupboard standby too – you'll need to use less of them as they're stronger than fresh herbs.

JARS AND BOTTLES
Artichokes Add to stews, traybakes, salads and pizza toppings.
Capers Great with fish, in pasta sauces, on pizzas, in salads and in tartare sauce.

Caramelised onion chutney Adds an extra layer of flavour to savoury tarts, galettes and the sausage rolls on page 68.

Cornichons and gherkins Use in salads and sandwiches for a great acidic crunch.

Hot sauce To add fiery heat to meat and cheese dishes, and just about anything else.

Olives Great in salads, pasta dishes, pizzas and traybakes.

Pickled chillies For instant heat and crunch in meat dishes, and with cheese.

Roasted red peppers Add these to pasta dishes, stews and traybakes for sweetness and colour.

Rose harissa To give an instant layer of heat and intensity, try coating veg, meat or fish with this before roasting.

Sesame oil For all kinds of Asian-style dishes and stir-fries.

Soy sauce Adds an intense umami taste to Asian-style dishes.

Tapenade This rich olive paste works as an instant base in pastry tarts. It also pairs well with meat and fish.

Tomato ketchup Not just to go with chips! I use this to add a sweet-sharp flavour to the sweet and sour sauce on page 76.

Mustard Each variety brings something different to a dish: English mustard has a clean fiery heat, Dijon has a mellower taste, wholegrain has a crunchy texture and I can't resist the bright yellow of sweet American mustard. A hint of mustard will enhance cheese dishes.

TINNED OR JARRED ANCHOVIES, SARDINES AND SMOKED MACKEREL

These are pure powerhouse ingredients which enable you to whip up flavoursome meals in minutes. Don't discard the oil in the tin – use it to cook the other ingredients for even more flavour. And don't be afraid of using anchovies in cooking – think of them like an intense seasoning.

SPICES I use dried spices in curries and spice rubs, and to add flavour to sauces and marinades, especially sweet smoked paprika, cumin, coriander and turmeric. I also like the mild aniseed taste of caraway seeds, which works brilliantly with pork. Saffron has an intense flavour and provides an amazing yellow colour. Nutmeg has an earthy versatility, which works in both sweet and savoury dishes.

SWEETNESS Dark chocolate, golden syrup, treacle, honey, vanilla bean paste and vanilla pods are perfect for boosting the flavour profile of puddings and cakes.

VINEGAR I tend to use cider vinegar and white and red wine vinegars for dressings, and rice vinegar for Asian-inspired dishes. Quick pickles, such as cucumber or shallots, are a clever way to add sharp freshness and balance any richness in dishes.

HAM & BACON QUICHE

A quiche done properly and served still slightly warm is a beautiful thing. The creamy custard mix will work with any fillings you choose – swap out the ham and bacon for broccoli, mushrooms, peas … whatever you have knocking about.

SERVES 8

500g pack ready-made shortcrust pastry

Plain flour, to dust

6 large free-range eggs, beaten

40g butter

200g bacon lardons

2 banana shallots, diced

1 tsp thyme leaves

125ml crème fraîche

100ml double cream

1 tsp Dijon mustard

60g Cheddar, grated

¼ fresh nutmeg, finely grated

2 tbsp finely chopped chives

120g thick sliced ham, diced

Salt and freshly ground black pepper

1. Have ready a loose-bottomed 25cm flan tin, 3.5cm deep. Lightly dust a large piece of baking paper with flour and roll out the pastry on the paper to a roughly 35cm circle, about 5mm thick. Gently lift the pastry into the flan tin, removing the paper (save this for later). Press it into the edges; leave a little overhanging the rim of the tin. Place in the fridge to firm up for 15 minutes. Meanwhile, preheat the oven to 200°C/Fan 180°C/Gas 6.

2. Take the pastry case from the fridge, prick the base all over with a fork and sit the tin on a baking sheet. Line the pastry case with the saved baking paper and add a layer of baking beans. Bake for 20 minutes, then remove the paper and beans. Brush the pastry case with a little of the beaten egg and then return the case to the oven for 15 minutes or until the pastry is a light golden brown. Leave to cool and then trim away the overhanging pastry with a sharp knife. Lower the oven setting to 190°C/Fan 170°C/Gas 5.

3. Melt the butter in a sauté pan over a medium-high heat. When it is foaming, add the lardons and cook for 4 minutes

or until starting to caramelise. Add the shallots and cook for 3–4 minutes to soften. Add the thyme and some seasoning, stir over the heat for 1 minute then remove and leave to cool.

4. Whisk the crème fraîche, cream, mustard, cheese, nutmeg and chives into the beaten eggs and season well. Spoon the bacon mix evenly into the pastry case, top with the ham and carefully pour on the egg mix. Bake on a high oven shelf for 25–30 minutes until golden and just set. Leave to cool in the tin for a few minutes, then remove and serve.

SPINACH & CHICKEN SALAD

This light but substantial spinach and chicken salad has the taste of Italian holidays all over it – white balsamic vinegar, pesto, cherry tomatoes, pine nuts and creamy buffalo mozzarella. Ready-cooked quinoa and ripe avocado are quick and easy ways to add texture and body to salads and are great ingredients to have on standby.

SERVES 2

2 skinless, boneless chicken breasts, sliced

4 tbsp extra virgin olive oil

2 tbsp pesto

1 tsp Dijon mustard

2 tbsp white balsamic vinegar

60g baby spinach leaves

½ red onion, finely sliced

150g cherry tomatoes, halved

250g pouch cooked red and white quinoa

½ ripe avocado, sliced

125g buffalo mozzarella, sliced

Salt and freshly ground black pepper

2 tbsp toasted pine nuts, to finish

1. Season the chicken with salt and pepper. Place a large non-stick frying pan over a high heat. When it is hot, add 1 tbsp olive oil and then lay the chicken slices in the pan. Cook for 2 minutes on each side or until the chicken is golden brown and cooked through. Remove from the heat and stir through the pesto.

2. To make the dressing, in a large bowl, whisk together the mustard, balsamic vinegar and remaining 3 tbsp extra virgin olive oil. Season with salt and pepper.

3. Add the spinach leaves, red onion, cherry tomatoes and quinoa to the bowl. Mix together well and then divide between 2 serving plates.

4. Add the avocado and mozzarella slices to the plates and top with the pesto chicken. Scatter over the toasted pine nuts and tuck in!

FOUR-CHEESE TOASTIE

Brilliantly gooey and melty Monterey Jack and mozzarella are perfect in these deluxe toasties, while Parmesan and blue cheese introduce a satisfying salty kick. Gruyère and Emmental are good oozy grilled-cheese options too. Pickled chillies are perfect with cheesy dishes like this, as they cut through the richness and give it all a lift.

SERVES 1

2 slices white bloomer

30g butter, softened

30g Parmesan, finely grated

2 tsp Dijon mustard

25g mozzarella, grated

25g Monterey Jack cheese, grated

25g blue cheese, crumbled

2 pickled chillies, sliced

Salt and freshly ground black pepper

1. Lay the bread slices on a board. Mix the softened butter and grated Parmesan together in a small bowl and set aside until needed.

2. Spread the Dijon mustard on one side of each bread slice. Sprinkle the mozzarella, Monterey Jack and blue cheese evenly on top of one mustard-topped bread slice and scatter over the pickled chilli slices. Season with a little salt and pepper. Press the second slice of bread on top of the filling, mustard side down.

3. Place a medium non-stick frying pan over a medium heat. Spread the top of the sandwich with half of the Parmesan butter and place in the pan, buttered side down. Spread the remaining Parmesan butter on top of the sandwich.

4. Cook for 3–4 minutes on each side or until the Parmesan turns a lovely golden brown and the cheese is oozing and melted on the inside. This is quite a decadent toastie so serve it with a crisp and zingy salad on the side if you want to balance it out a bit!

POTATO & COURGETTE HASH BROWNS

Potato and courgette hash browns are delicious on their own, but serve them with crispy bacon and a fried egg and they become a real brunch or lunchtime treat. Grating and salting the veg beforehand draws out some of the moisture, which means it won't go mushy as it cooks.

SERVES 2

1 small onion, grated

1 large courgette (180g), julienned

1 potato (150g), julienned

1 garlic clove, finely grated

1 large free-range egg

1 tsp thyme leaves

30g Parmesan, finely grated

4 tbsp cornflour

1 tbsp olive oil

10g butter

Salt and freshly ground black pepper

1. Put the onion, courgette and potato into a large bowl. Sprinkle liberally with salt and mix well with your hands. Leave the mixture to sit for 5 minutes. Next, tip the mixture onto a J-cloth or piece of muslin and squeeze out all the liquid from the vegetables.

2. Tip the mixture into a clean bowl and season with some pepper. Add the garlic, egg, thyme and Parmesan and mix well. Sprinkle the cornflour over the mixture, mix to combine thoroughly and form into 4 equal-sized patties.

3. Place a large non-stick frying pan over a medium-high heat and add the olive oil and butter. When the butter is melted and foaming, add the patties to the pan and fry for 3–4 minutes on each side or until crispy and cooked through.

4. Transfer the hash browns to warmed plates. Serve a fried egg and crisp-fried bacon rashers on the side if you like.

MACKEREL WITH BEETROOT & KOHLRABI

Mackerel is a great sustainable fish that I think we should all be eating more of. The quick pickles add a sweet and sour crunch to balance the earthy flavours of the veg and creamy, mustardy dressing. If you can't find kohlrabi, use cabbage instead.

SERVES 2

150g kohlrabi, julienned

50g cooked beetroot, julienned

1 tbsp mayonnaise

1 tbsp Greek yoghurt

1 tsp wholegrain mustard

4 cornichons, sliced

½ tsp cider vinegar

1 tbsp flat-leaf parsley, finely chopped

4 mackerel fillets, pin-boned

1 tbsp olive oil

Salt and freshly ground black pepper

PICKLED VEG

6 radishes, finely sliced

½ candy beetroot, halved and finely sliced

4 tbsp cider vinegar

2 tsp caster sugar

1. First prepare the pickled veg. Pop the radishes and candy beetroot into a small heatproof bowl. Put the cider vinegar and sugar into a small saucepan and stir over a medium heat until the sugar dissolves then pour over the radishes and beetroot. Set aside to pickle.

2. In a medium bowl, mix the kohlrabi and beetroot julienne with the mayonnaise, yoghurt, mustard, cornichons, cider vinegar and chopped parsley. Season with a little salt and pepper to taste.

3. Pat the mackerel fillets dry and season on both sides with salt and pepper. Place a large non-stick frying pan over a medium heat. Add the olive oil and when it's hot, place the mackerel fillets in the pan, skin side down. Press them down firmly for around 5 seconds to prevent the skin from curling and cook for 2 minutes on each side.

4. While the fish is cooking, drain the pickled veg well. Once it is cooked, remove the mackerel from the pan and place a couple of fillets on each serving plate. Pile the kohlrabi and beetroot salad alongside and add a generous spoonful of pickled beetroot and radishes to each plate.

CARROT FRITTERS WITH HERBY YOGHURT

These crunchy fritters are a perfect speedy lunch. Carrots bring sweetness and there's gentle spicing from the nigella seeds and cumin, all cooled down with a herby yoghurt dip. Once you've got the hang of making the fritters, play around with the ingredients you use – any root veg, or courgettes, will work.

MAKES 16–20

500g grated carrots

2 large free-range eggs, beaten

1 tsp nigella (black onion) seeds

1 tsp ground cumin

4 spring onions, finely sliced

3 tbsp flat-leaf parsley, finely chopped

6 tbsp plain flour

4 tbsp finely grated Parmesan

50ml vegetable or sunflower oil, to cook

Salt and freshly ground black pepper

Lemon wedges, to serve

HERBY YOGHURT

250g Greek yoghurt

Juice of ½ lemon

1 small garlic clove, finely grated

2 tbsp mint leaves, finely chopped

2 tbsp dill leaves, chopped

1. Put the grated carrots into the middle of a clean J-cloth or tea towel and squeeze to remove as much liquid as possible. Tip the carrots into a large bowl.

2. Add the beaten eggs, spices, spring onions, parsley, flour and grated Parmesan to the carrots and season generously with salt and pepper. Mix with your hands or a wooden spoon until well combined. (Now this mixture can hold in the fridge until you are ready to cook the fritters.)

3. For the herby yoghurt, mix all the ingredients together in a bowl and season with salt and pepper to taste. Set aside.

4. Place a large non-stick frying pan over a medium-high heat. When it is hot, add the oil and let it heat up. Test the oil by putting a tiny bit of the carrot mixture into the pan; if bubbles form around it, the oil is ready.

5. You will need to cook the fritters in batches. Add heaped tablespoonfuls of the carrot mixture to the pan. Cook for 3–4 minutes or until crisp and golden brown on each side, flattening each one a little with the back of the spoon before flipping it over.

6. As the fritters are cooked, pop them on a baking tray and keep them warm in a low oven, while you cook the rest.

7. Once they are all cooked, pop the fritters onto plates and add a big spoonful of herby yoghurt. Serve with lemon wedges, and a side salad if you like.

CORNED BEEF & POTATO HAND PIES

These little hand pies use a retro store-cupboard ingredient: corned beef. I love corned beef – it's tasty, cheap and acts like a fantastic flavour binder. Every mouthful of golden pie is packed with interest from the chunky filling. *Pictured overleaf*

MAKES 6

350g potatoes, peeled and diced

20g butter

1 tbsp mild olive oil

1 onion, diced

340g tin corned beef, cut into large dice

100g gherkins, roughly chopped

2 tsp dried mixed herbs

½ tsp ground mace

2 tsp Dijon mustard

1 tbsp Worcestershire sauce

3 tbsp flat-leaf parsley, chopped

2 x 340g packs ready-rolled shortcrust pastry

2 tbsp plain flour, to dust

1 large free-range egg, lightly beaten with a pinch of salt

Salt and freshly ground black pepper

1. Put the potatoes into a small pan, add water to cover and salt. Bring to the boil then simmer for around 10 minutes, until the potatoes are just tender. Drain in a sieve; set aside.

2. Heat the butter and olive oil in a sauté pan over a high heat. Add the onion and sauté for 4–5 minutes until soft and caramelising at the edges. Add the corned beef and potatoes and cook for 2 minutes, breaking up the corned beef and mashing some of the potato with the back of the spoon.

3. Add the gherkins, dried herbs, mace and a little salt and pepper. Stir well, then check the seasoning. Remove from the heat and let cool slightly, then stir in the mustard, Worcestershire sauce and parsley. Leave to cool completely.

4. Line 2 baking trays with baking paper. Unroll both packs of shortcrust pastry and cut each one down the middle lengthways. Cut each piece into 3 equal squares, so you have 12 in total. Lay 6 squares on the lined baking trays.

5. Lightly dust your work surface with flour then gently roll the remaining 6 pastry squares so that they are a bit bigger and a touch thinner. (These will be the top layers and need to be a bit larger to cover the filling with ease.) Pop them onto another tray and place both trays in the fridge to rest the pastry until the filling has cooled down.

6. To assemble the pies, brush the edges of the bottom pastry squares with beaten egg. Divide the filling between these squares, piling it into the middle. Place the rolled-out squares on top and press the edges together to seal. Pop these back into the fridge to firm up.

7. Meanwhile, preheat the oven to 200°C/Fan 180°C/Gas 6. Take the pies from the fridge and press the edges with a fork to seal firmly, then trim to neaten, using a sharp knife. Brush the pastry with beaten egg and make a few slashes in the top to allow the steam to escape. Bake for about 25 minutes until golden brown. Enjoy the pies while they are still warm.

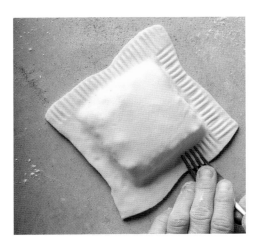

SESAME SALMON, MANGO & BROWN RICE POKE BOWL

There is so much going on in this colourful lunch bowl – crunchy carrots, edamame beans and peppery radishes, juicy mango, fresh herbs and a sticky Asian-style glaze on the salmon. You want to cook the fish nice and gently. Don't worry about under-doing it as you can eat salmon when it's still a bit pink inside.

SERVES 2

2 skinless salmon fillets (125g each)

2 tbsp soy sauce

3 tbsp mirin

1–2 x 250g pouches cooked brown rice, depending on appetite

100g peeled mango, diced

1 tbsp coriander leaves, finely chopped

80g edamame beans

1 tbsp vegetable or sunflower oil

PICKLED VEG

80g carrot, julienned

6 radishes, thinly sliced

60ml white wine vinegar

2 tsp caster sugar

TO FINISH

1 tbsp toasted sesame seeds

1. Cut each salmon fillet into 3 equal-sized pieces. Place the pieces in a shallow bowl and pour over the soy and mirin. Mix well and set aside to marinate for 20 minutes.

2. Meanwhile, prepare your pickled veg. Pop the carrot and radishes into a heatproof bowl. Put the wine vinegar and sugar into a small saucepan over a medium-high heat and stir until the sugar dissolves then pour over the carrot and radishes. Leave to pickle for 15 minutes.

3. Heat up the brown rice and divide between two warmed serving bowls. Mix the mango with the chopped coriander and add to the bowls. Pile the edamame beans alongside. Drain the pickles and add these too.

4. Place a small non-stick frying pan over a medium heat. Add the oil then, when it's hot, add the salmon pieces to the pan; reserve the marinade. Cook for 4–5 minutes, turning the pieces to cook evenly. (Don't increase the heat or the soy and mirin coating may burn.) Divide the salmon between the serving bowls.

5. Place the pan back on the heat, pour in the reserved marinade and let it bubble for a minute to reduce to a sticky glaze. Spoon this over the salmon, sprinkle with the toasted sesame seeds and serve.

STEAK & SALAD WITH BLUE CHEESE DRESSING

Salty, tangy blue cheese and rich, juicy steak are such an incredible pairing. It's quite a sophisticated flavour combination, so this probably isn't one for the kids, but that's alright – let's keep it for the grown-ups.

SERVES 2

2 sirloin steaks (200g each)

1 tbsp vegetable oil

Salt and freshly ground black pepper

DRESSING

2 tbsp soured cream

2 tbsp mayonnaise

1 tbsp crumbled blue cheese

1 tsp American mustard

½ tsp white wine vinegar

A few dashes of hot sauce

SALAD

2 Little Gem lettuce

100g green beans, blanched and halved

125g cherry tomatoes, halved

8 radishes, quartered

6 cornichons, thickly sliced

TO FINISH

2 tbsp crumbled blue cheese

A few chives, chopped

1. Take your sirloin steaks out of the fridge about 15 minutes before you intend to cook them (to get them closer to room temperature for even cooking). Season both sides well with salt and pepper and rub with the oil.

2. Place a large non-stick frying pan over a high heat. When it is smoking, carefully add the sirloin steaks, holding them fat side down with a pair of tongs for around a minute or until the fat has crisped up well.

3. Now lay the steaks flat in the frying pan and cook for 2–3 minutes on each side (they will still be nice and pink in the middle). Remove the steaks from the pan and transfer to a warmed plate. Set aside to rest while you prepare the rest of the salad.

4. Mix all the dressing ingredients together in a small bowl and season with a little salt and pepper to taste.

5. Separate the lettuce leaves and halve them lengthways. Divide the lettuce, green beans, cherry tomatoes, radishes and cornichons evenly between your serving plates. Scatter over the crumbled blue cheese and season with a little salt and pepper.

6. Pour the resting juices from the steaks into the salad dressing and stir well, then spoon over the salad. Slice the steak and lay it on top of the salad. Sprinkle with the chopped chives to serve.

RAREBIT CRUMPETS

When you're making Welsh rarebit you want strong flavours to drive through every layer. Choose a good mature Cheddar that will hold up against the two types of mustard, Worcestershire sauce and stout. Using a crumpet as the base makes this a bit more special, but it'll work on regular sliced white too.

MAKES 4

30g butter

40g plain flour

200ml Guinness or stout

1 tsp English mustard

1 tsp Dijon mustard

1 tsp Worcestershire sauce

150g Cheddar, grated

1 free-range egg yolk

4 crumpets

120g sliced ham

Salt and freshly ground black pepper

Watercress or rocket salad, to serve

1. Preheat the oven to 180°C/Gas 4 with the grill element turned on.

2. Melt the butter in a saucepan over a medium heat, then tip in the flour and cook, stirring with a wooden spoon, for 2 minutes. Swap the spoon for a whisk. Gradually pour in the stout, whisking well after each addition. Cook, whisking gently for a few minutes, or until the mixture thickens.

3. Remove the pan from the heat and stir in both mustards, the Worcestershire sauce and grated Cheddar. Stir well until the cheese is fully melted. Taste for seasoning, adding some pepper and salt if needed, then stir in the egg yolk and leave to cool slightly.

4. Now toast your crumpets then place on a baking tray. Lay some ham on top of each one. Spoon over the cheesy sauce and flatten the mixture down slightly. Place on a high oven shelf under the grill for 5–8 minutes until golden.

5. Remove the tray from the oven and leave the crumpets to cool down for a couple of minutes before tucking in. Serve with a little watercress or rocket salad on the side.

PEA & KALE BUBBLE & SQUEAK

I love kale, with its dark, irony structure, and think it goes brilliantly with the sweetness of peas and the light, fragrant basil leaves in these patties. Bubble and squeak is a really old-school way of using up leftovers, but it's easy to make from scratch too.

MAKES 4

300g mashed potato (leftover or freshly cooked)

50g frozen peas

2 tbsp olive oil

30g butter

2 banana shallots, finely diced

50g kale, roughly chopped

1 large free-range egg, beaten

2 tbsp basil leaves, finely chopped

20g Parmesan, finely grated

2 large tomatoes

½ tsp dried oregano

20g plain flour

Salt and freshly ground black pepper

TO SERVE

Avocado slices

2 poached (or fried) free-range eggs (optional)

1. Put the mashed potato and peas into a large bowl and season with little salt and pepper. Set aside.

2. Heat half the olive oil and half the butter in a large non-stick frying pan over a medium heat. When the butter is melted, add the shallots and cook until softened. Then stir through the kale and cook until tender.

3. Tip the contents of the pan into the bowl of mashed potato and peas. Leave to cool slightly, then add the egg, basil and Parmesan and mix well. Form the mixture into 4 equal-sized patties and place in the fridge for 15 minutes to firm up. (You can prepare the patties ahead to this point and keep them in the fridge, ready to cook.)

4. Cut the tomatoes in half, then cut a thin sliver off the base of each half with a sharp knife, so they can sit level. Sprinkle with the oregano and some salt and pepper.

5. Dust your patties with flour on both sides. Place the frying pan back on the heat, add the remaining olive oil and butter and heat until the butter is melted and foaming. Now add the patties to the pan, along with the tomatoes, and cook for 2–3 minutes on each side until browned.

6. Transfer the pea and kale patties and the tomatoes to warmed plates and arrange some avocado slices on top of the tomatoes. I usually have them with poached (or fried) eggs, too.

MAPLE & SOY CHICKEN RICE BOWL

In this super-tasty chicken and rice bowl, soy sauce, maple syrup and mirin bring their big, powerful Asian flavours to the sticky glaze coating the chicken. Using lots of items you can keep in your store-cupboard, this is a great quick lunch.

SERVES 2

4 boneless chicken thighs (skin on)

1 tsp vegetable oil

2 tbsp soy sauce

3 tbsp cloudy apple juice

2 tbsp mirin

1 garlic clove, finely grated

2 tbsp maple syrup

1 tsp rice vinegar

4 tbsp water

1 tsp cornflour mixed to a paste with 1 tbsp water

1–2 x 250g pouches cooked jasmine rice, depending on appetite

Salt and white pepper

2 spring onions, finely shredded, to finish

1. Season both side of the chicken thighs with salt and white pepper. Place a medium non-stick frying pan over a low to medium heat. When hot, add the oil and then place the chicken thighs in the pan, skin side down. Cook gently for around 10–15 minutes, so that the fat is slowly rendered from the skin and you end up with nice crispy skin. Make sure you use a non-stick pan so that they don't stick!

2. Meanwhile, mix the soy sauce, apple juice, mirin, garlic, maple syrup, rice vinegar and water together in a small bowl to make a sauce; set aside.

3. When the chicken is cooked on the skin side and it's nice and crispy, turn each thigh over and cook for 2 minutes on the other side. Remove the chicken from the pan and set aside on a plate.

4. Add the sauce to the frying pan and let it simmer for 1–2 minutes. Add the chicken back to the pan, placing it skin side up, and stir in the blended cornflour, Cook, stirring, for another 2 minutes until the sauce is thickened.

5. Heat up the jasmine rice and place in warmed serving bowls. Remove the chicken from the sauce, slice it thickly and place on top of the rice. Spoon over the sauce, sprinkle with spring onions and enjoy!

TOMATO & OLIVE PUFF PASTRY TART

It's no secret that I love Greek food and with tomatoes, olives, oregano and feta this tart is a real nod to Greek cookery. You can play around with the toppings – try different cheeses, ham or caramelised onion jam, or make it pizza-like with mozzarella, anchovies or pepperoni. Keep a roll of puff pastry in the freezer and you're always ready to go.

SERVES 4

320g pack ready-rolled all-butter puff pastry

1 large free-range egg, beaten with a pinch of salt

5 tbsp black olive tapenade

500g tomatoes (ideally a mix of heirloom and cherry tomatoes), large tomatoes thickly sliced, cherry tomatoes halved

2 tbsp oregano leaves

100g feta, crumbled

Salt and freshly ground black pepper

PICKLED SHALLOT

1 banana shallot, thinly sliced into rings

100ml white wine vinegar

2 tbsp golden caster sugar

TO FINISH

Extra virgin olive oil, to drizzle

1. Preheat the oven to 210°C/Fan 190°C/Gas 6½. Line a baking tray with baking paper.

2. Unravel the puff pastry and roll out to a slightly thinner large rectangle. Transfer to the lined tray. Make small folds around the edge of the pastry by folding the edge of the pastry inwards, using your fingertip and pressing down, to create a slightly thicker pastry rim. Do this all the way round.

3. Using a small sharp knife, score a line around the pastry just inside the rim. Pierce the entire base of the pastry well. Brush the pastry, including the folded rim, with beaten egg and bake on a high shelf in the oven for 15 minutes.

4. Meanwhile, for the pickled shallot, put the shallot rings into a heatproof bowl. Heat the wine vinegar and sugar in a small pan over a medium heat, stir until the sugar dissolves then pour over the shallot. Leave to pickle for 15 minutes.

5. When the pastry is cooked, remove from the oven and leave to cool down slightly. If the middle part has risen, press it down with the back of a spoon.

6. Spread the tapenade over the pastry and arrange the tomatoes on top. Sprinkle evenly with the oregano and feta. Season with a little salt and pepper and bake on a high shelf in the oven for 15 minutes.

7. As you remove the tart from the oven, drizzle with a little extra virgin olive oil. Scatter over the pickled shallot and serve, with a leafy salad on the side.

MACKEREL & BROCCOLI FISH CAKES

Fish cakes are ideal for using up bits and bobs. Feel free to change the herbs, or use chopped kale or cauliflower in place of broccoli. The smoked mackerel gives a rich flavour and beautiful texture, but be careful not to overwork the mixture.

SERVES 4

1 tbsp mild olive oil, plus extra to fry

40g butter, plus extra to fry

1 red onion, diced

2 garlic cloves, finely chopped

½ head broccoli, including the stalk (275g)

2 tbsp rosemary leaves, finely chopped

1 tbsp sage leaves, finely chopped

300g pack British smoked mackerel fillets, skinned

500g mashed potato (leftover or freshly cooked)

1 large free-range egg, beaten

100g feta, crumbled

Finely grated zest of 1 lemon

50g plain flour

Salt and freshly ground black pepper

TO SERVE

Lemon wedges

Mixed leaf salad

1. Heat the olive oil and butter in a large non-stick frying pan over a medium-high heat. Add the onion and cook, stirring, for 3 minutes. Add the garlic and cook for another 2 minutes.

2. While the onion is cooking, break off the florets from the broccoli stem and thinly slice them; set aside. Cut the stalk in half lengthways and then slice it quite thinly.

3. Add the sliced broccoli stalk to the frying pan and cook for 2 minutes, then add the sliced florets, along with the herbs. Cook for a few minutes or until the broccoli is tender. Remove from the heat and leave to cool completely.

4. Meanwhile, flake the smoked mackerel, checking for pin bones and discarding any dark grey flesh. Put the flaked mackerel into a bowl and add the mashed potato, egg, feta and lemon zest, along with the cooled broccoli mixture and plenty of salt and pepper. Mix well with your hands.

5. Divide the mixture into 8 portions and shape into patties. Place on a tray in the fridge for 20 minutes or so, to firm up. (You can make them ahead to this point; keep in the fridge, ready to cook.) Preheat the oven to 180°C/Fan 160°C/Gas 4.

6. Dust the fish cakes lightly with flour on both sides. Place a large non-stick frying pan over a medium-high heat and add 1–2 tbsp oil and a knob of butter. When hot, add 4 fish cakes and cook for 3–4 minutes on each side until golden then transfer to a baking tray. Repeat to cook the remaining fish cakes. Pop the tray into the oven for 10 minutes or so to ensure the fish cakes are warmed through.

7. Serve the fish cakes with lemon wedges and a leafy salad.

CHEDDAR SAUSAGE ROLLS

Warm from the oven, these quick and easy sausage rolls will do your lunchtime proud. It's all about getting as much extra flavour as possible into the sausage meat with Cheddar, caramelised onion chutney and fresh thyme. Go ahead and have a dollop of brown sauce on the side if you fancy it too.

MAKES 6

500g pork sausages, outer skins removed

2 tsp thyme leaves

3 tbsp caramelised onion chutney

130g Cheddar, grated

320g pack ready-rolled all-butter puff pastry

1 large free-range egg, lightly beaten with a pinch of salt

Salt and freshly ground black pepper

1. Put the sausage meat into a bowl with the thyme, chutney and 100g of the grated cheese. Season the mixture with salt and pepper and mix well.

2. Unroll the puff pastry and lay it out flat on your work surface. Cut it in half, to give two 23 x 18cm rectangles. Divide the sausage mixture in half and roll each portion into an even sausage shape, 23cm long. Place a sausage filling roll down the middle of each pastry rectangle and press it down lightly.

3. Brush the pastry on either side of the sausage filling with beaten egg. Now lift the pastry from the right side over the filling and then lift the left side over that. Flip the long sausage roll over so that the folded side is now on the bottom. Place this on a tray lined with baking paper and repeat with the other sausage filling and pastry.

4. Put both sausage rolls in the freezer to firm up for at least 30 minutes. Preheat the oven to 200°C/Fan 180°C/Gas 6.

5. When the rolls are semi-frozen, cut each into 3 even-sized lengths. Brush the undersides with beaten egg, then turn them top side up. Brush with beaten egg and sprinkle with the remaining cheese. (You can make them ahead to this point and keep them in the fridge, ready to cook.)

6. Place the sausage rolls on a lined baking tray and bake on a high shelf in the oven for 25 minutes. The pastry should be deep golden brown and the filling cooked through and piping hot. Let them cool down for a few minutes before tucking in.

TEA

CREAM OF CHICKEN SOUP

Chicken soup with thick slices of crusty bread is such a comforting, wholesome meal. What really elevates it here is the fresh herbs: tarragon and chicken are a beautiful match, and parsley gives it a lovely earthy freshness.

SERVES 4

800g chicken thighs (skin on and bone in)

40g butter

1 onion, diced

2 leeks, washed, halved lengthways and sliced

4 celery sticks, diced

2 garlic cloves, thinly sliced

200ml white wine

800ml chicken stock

100ml double cream, plus an extra 4 tbsp to finish

1 tbsp tarragon leaves, finely chopped

¼ nutmeg, finely grated

Salt and freshly ground black pepper

1 tbsp chopped flat-leaf parsley, to finish

1. Season both sides of the chicken thighs well with salt and pepper. Add half the butter to a large non-stick sauté pan and place over a medium-high heat. When the butter is melted and foaming, add the chicken thighs, placing them skin side down in the pan. Cook for 3–4 minutes on each side or until sealed and golden brown on each side. Remove with a slotted spoon and set aside on a plate.

2. Add the remaining butter to the pan. Once melted, add the onion, leeks and celery and sauté gently for 5–6 minutes or until softened. Add the sliced garlic and cook for a further 2 minutes. Increase the heat to high, pour in the wine and let it bubble until reduced by half.

3. Add the chicken stock to the pan, along with the browned chicken thighs. Bring to a simmer, put the lid on and simmer gently for 20 minutes. Take the pan off the heat and lift the chicken thighs out onto a plate to cool down.

4. When the chicken is cool enough to handle, remove and discard the skin and tear the meat from the bones. Shred the chicken meat and add half of it back to the pan.

5. Now blitz the soup in a jug blender until smooth. Pour this back into the pan and add the cream and tarragon. Bring back to a simmer and season the soup with the nutmeg and salt and pepper to taste.

6. Divide the chicken soup between warmed bowls and add a generous drizzle of cream. Top with the remaining shredded chicken and finish with a scattering of parsley. Enjoy with some crusty bread.

PANTRY SPAGHETTI

You can rustle up this easy pasta dish using ingredients you probably already have in your store-cupboard and fridge. Big strong flavours from anchovies, garlic and chilli are transformed into an amazing sauce using some of the starchy pasta cooking water and lots of freshly grated Parmesan.

SERVES 1

120g dried spaghetti

1 tbsp extra virgin olive oil

2 garlic cloves, sliced

2 tinned anchovy fillets

A pinch of dried chilli flakes

2 tbsp flat-leaf parsley
(or basil or chives), finely
chopped

20g Parmesan, finely grated

A knob of butter (10g)

Salt and freshly ground
black pepper

1. Half-fill a medium saucepan with boiling water, add salt and place over a high heat. Add your spaghetti to the boiling water and stir it gently as it softens. (The reason for the smaller amount of water than usual is so that it will have a greater concentration of starch from the pasta; this starch will help emulsify your sauce.)

2. Place a medium frying pan over a medium heat and add the olive oil. When the pan begins to heat up, toss in the garlic and let it sizzle gently for a minute or so. Add the anchovies and stir, so they melt into the oil. Add the chilli flakes and check on your pasta – you want it to be *al dente* or 'just cooked'.

3. When the spaghetti is cooked, use tongs to lift it from the saucepan and place it directly in the frying pan. Add a good half-ladleful of pasta water too. Sprinkle in the chopped parsley and Parmesan and toss the pasta until the sauce starts to emulsify, then add the butter. Taste to check the seasoning, adding pepper and salt if needed.

4. Transfer the spaghetti to a warmed bowl, add a little more Parmesan, if you like, and tuck in straight away.

SWEET & SOUR PRAWN STIR-FRY

Tiger prawns make quick stir-fries feel a bit more special. This has all the taste and texture of a classic sweet and sour: lightly battered prawns, chunky peppers, red onion and pineapple chunks. You can try it with small strips of chicken breast too.

SERVES 2

300g large tiger prawns, peeled and deveined (tails left on)

1 tbsp soy sauce

1 large free-range egg, lightly beaten

50g cornflour

Vegetable or sunflower oil, to shallow-fry

SWEET AND SOUR SAUCE

2 tbsp caster sugar

2 tbsp tomato ketchup

2 tbsp rice vinegar

3 tbsp pineapple juice

1 tbsp soy sauce

4 tbsp water

½ red onion, chopped

1 garlic clove, finely chopped

½ red pepper, cut into large dice

½ green pepper, cut into large dice

12 tinned pineapple chunks

1 tsp cornflour, mixed to a paste with 1 tbsp water

1. Pat the tiger prawns dry with kitchen paper. Mix the soy sauce, egg and cornflour together in a medium bowl to a smooth batter. Add the prawns and turn to coat in the batter. Heat a 3–5cm depth of oil in a medium saucepan to about 180°C (check with a thermometer).

2. While the oil is heating up, for the sweet and sour sauce, mix the sugar, ketchup, rice vinegar, pineapple juice, soy sauce and water together in a small bowl. Set aside.

3. You will need to cook the prawns in a couple of batches. When the oil is hot, take half of the prawns from the batter and carefully lower them into the oil. Cook for 1–2 minutes on each side, then remove with a slotted spoon and place on a tray lined with kitchen paper to absorb any excess oil. Repeat to cook the rest of the prawns.

4. Place a large frying pan or wok over a high heat. Take 1 tbsp of the shallow-frying oil and add it to the pan. When it is hot, add the onion and garlic and stir-fry for 1 minute. Toss in the peppers and cook for another minute, then add the pineapple chunks and sweet and sour sauce mixture. Stir well.

5. Add the prawns back to the pan, along with the blended cornflour. Cook, stirring, for another 2 minutes or until the sauce thickens and the prawns are warmed through. Serve immediately, with jasmine rice.

VEGETABLE BAJEE BURGERS

Crunchy and spicy, topped with fresh mint yoghurt, mango chutney and a sprinkle of Bombay mix, these veggie bajees are an amazing meat-free alternative on burger night. They also make a delicious side for any curry dish.

SERVES 4

1 onion, finely sliced

1 tsp salt

1 tsp chilli powder

1 tsp ground turmeric

1 tsp ground coriander

2 carrots, julienned (150g)

2 courgettes, julienned (200g)

50g spinach, roughly chopped

200g gram (chickpea) flour

Vegetable or sunflower oil, to shallow-fry

MINTY YOGHURT

200ml natural yoghurt

3 tbsp mint leaves, finely chopped

A pinch of salt

TO ASSEMBLE

4 burger buns, split

4–6 tbsp Bombay mix

4 handfuls of mixed salad leaves

4 tbsp mango chutney

1. Put the onion, salt and ground spices into a large bowl and mix really well with your hands for around 1–2 minutes, squeezing as you go. (The salt draws out moisture from the onions and this will help the flour to hold the bajees together.) Add the carrot and courgette julienne and continue to mix and squeeze with your hands.

2. Add the chopped spinach and gram flour and mix until evenly combined – the mixture should be quite firm.

3. Preheat the oven to 180°C/Fan 160°C/Gas 4. Heat a 4cm depth of oil in a sauté pan. Meanwhile, in a small bowl, mix the yoghurt with the mint and salt. Set aside.

4. You will need to cook the vegetable bajees a few at a time to maintain the oil at a constant temperature. When the oil is hot, take tablespoonfuls of the bajee mix and carefully drop into the sauté pan, spacing them well apart and slightly flattening them as you do so. Cook for 2–3 minutes on each side, then remove the bajees with a slotted spoon and drain on kitchen paper.

5. Transfer the cooked bajees to a metal rack set over a baking tray and pop them into the oven to keep warm while you cook the rest of the mixture. You should be able to make 12–16 bajees in total.

6. To assemble, lightly toast the burger buns. Spread the bases with minty yoghurt and top with a couple of crispy bajees. Sprinkle over some Bombay mix and add a handful of salad leaves. Spread the burger lids with mango chutney, pop on top of the burgers and press lightly. Serve at once.

SAUSAGE TRAYBAKE WITH HONEY MUSTARD GLAZE

Traybakes are the king of stress-free cooking. With crisped-up new potatoes, roasted cabbage and chunky sausages, this is your meat and two veg all cooked in one. Get yourself some good-quality bangers – you could even try some spicy merguez sausages if you'd like a bit of heat.

SERVES 4

750g medium new potatoes

1 tbsp olive oil

1 tbsp rosemary leaves, finely chopped

8 pork sausages

1 white cabbage, cut into 8 wedges

20g butter, melted

6 baby leeks, cut into 4cm lengths

1 whole garlic bulb, halved through the equator

1–2 tbsp thyme leaves

Salt and freshly ground black pepper

GLAZE

300ml beef stock

2 tbsp wholegrain mustard

2 tbsp honey

1 tbsp red wine vinegar

1 tsp cornflour, mixed to a paste with 1 tbsp water

1 tbsp flat-leaf parsley, finely chopped

1. Preheat the oven to 220°C/Fan 200°C/Gas 7. Add the new potatoes to a pan of boiling salted water, bring to the boil and cook for 10–12 minutes or until just tender. Drain well.

2. Place the boiled new potatoes in a large roasting tray and smash each one to flatten, using the base of a coffee mug or a sturdy glass. Drizzle over the olive oil, sprinkle with the rosemary and season generously with salt and pepper. Mix with your hands, making sure the potatoes are well coated with the oil. Bake on a high shelf in the oven for 15 minutes.

3. Take the tray from the oven and flip each potato over. Add the sausages and cabbage wedges to the tray, brushing the exposed sides of the cabbage with melted butter to stop them drying out. Add the baby leeks and halved garlic bulb.

4. Place the tray back in the oven on the middle shelf and bake for 15 minutes. Take the tray out again and turn the sausages and veg. Return to the oven for a final 15 minutes.

5. While the traybake finishes cooking, make the glaze. Put the beef stock, mustard and honey into a small saucepan and bring to a simmer, stirring, over a medium-high heat. Add the wine vinegar and a little seasoning. Stir in the blended cornflour and cook, stirring, until the glaze thickens slightly. Taste to check the seasoning and remove from the heat. Stir through the chopped parsley.

6. Take the sausage traybake from the oven and trickle the honey mustard glaze over everything. Serve straight away, with some crusty bread alongside.

BETH'S HIDE-THE-VEG BOLOGNESE

If you have fussy eaters to feed, this is a great way of getting plenty of vegetables into them without them really knowing. Use a food processor to make light work of chopping up whatever you have floating around in your fridge, then cook it in with the smoky pancetta and minced beef. A good one to batch up and freeze.

SERVES 4–6

1 large onion, quartered

2 large carrots, cut into large chunks

3 celery sticks, cut into 5cm pieces

3 garlic cloves, peeled

1 large courgette

200g mushrooms

3 tbsp olive oil

150g smoked pancetta, cubed

500g beef mince (12% fat)

2 tbsp tomato purée

200ml red wine

300ml beef stock

700ml jar passata

100ml water

1 tsp dried oregano

Salt and freshly ground black pepper

TO SERVE

Pasta of your choice

Finely grated Parmesan

1. Put the onion, carrots, celery and garlic into a food processor and pulse in short bursts to chop the vegetables finely. Remove and set aside in a bowl. Add the courgette and mushrooms to the food processor and pulse to chop these finely too. Set aside in another bowl.

2. Heat half of the olive oil in a large non-stick casserole pan over a medium-high heat. Add the pancetta and sauté for around 5 minutes, until it begins to turn brown and crispy. Remove with a slotted spoon and set aside on a plate.

3. Increase the heat under your pan to high and add the beef mince. Break it up quickly with a wooden spoon and cook, stirring, for 10–12 minutes until well browned. Remove the beef from the pan and set aside on a plate. Place the pan back on a medium-high heat.

4. Add the remaining olive oil to the pan. When it's hot, add the onion, carrot and celery mixture to the pan and sauté for 3–4 minutes or until the veg are tender.

5. Add the courgette and mushroom mix to the pan and cook over a high heat until tender and the liquid released by the vegetables is driven off.

6. Now add the beef and pancetta back into the pan, along with the tomato purée. Cook over a high heat, stirring from time to time, for 2 minutes. Deglaze the pan with the wine, stirring and scraping up any sticky bits from the bottom. Let the wine bubble until reduced by half.

7. Add the beef stock and passata to the pan. Pour the water into the empty passata jar and swish it around to clean out the jar, then pour that into the pan too and stir well. Bring to the boil then reduce the heat to a simmer. Cook for about 30 minutes, stirring every 10 minutes. Taste the sauce and add some salt and pepper to it.

8. Serve the bolognese sauce with your favourite pasta and lots of Parmesan cheese.

MINCED BEEF & ONION POT PIES

These individual pies look amazing and taste even better, yet they are easy to prepare, using ready-made puff pastry. Take your time to properly brown the meat so it caramelises and gets super-tasty. You can prepare the filling well ahead.

SERVES 4

2 tbsp olive oil

2 large onions, finely diced

500g beef mince (12% fat)

2 garlic cloves, finely chopped

1 tbsp thyme leaves

1 tbsp tomato purée

2½ tbsp plain flour

500ml beef stock

1 tsp Marmite

½ tsp sugar

1 tbsp Worcestershire sauce

1½ x 320g packs ready-rolled all-butter puff pastry

1 free-range egg, lightly beaten with a pinch of salt, to glaze

Salt and freshly ground black pepper

1. Heat half the olive oil in a large non-stick sauté pan over a medium-high heat. When it is hot, add the onions and cook for 5 minutes or until softened and starting to caramelise. Remove from the pan with a slotted spoon and set aside.

2. Place the pan back over a high heat and add the remaining olive oil. When the pan is smoking hot, add the beef to the pan, break it up quickly with a wooden spoon and cook, stirring, for 10–12 minutes until well browned.

3. Return the onions to the pan, add the garlic and thyme and cook for 2 minutes. Stir in the tomato purée and cook for another 2 minutes, then sprinkle in the flour. Cook, stirring, for 1–2 minutes, then gradually stir in the beef stock. Add the Marmite and sugar and bring to the boil. Cook for about 5 minutes or until the gravy thickens a little.

4. Remove from the heat and stir in the Worcestershire sauce. Season with salt and pepper to taste. Spoon the beef mixture into 4 individual pot pie dishes, dividing it equally, and leave to cool.

5. Meanwhile, preheat the oven to 200°C/Fan 180°C/Gas 6.

6. Once the filling is cooled, unroll the puff pastry and cut 4 circles, slightly larger than the top of the pie dishes. Brush the edges with beaten egg and position the circles (glazed edges down) over the filling. Press the edges onto the rim of the dishes to seal and brush the top of the pastry with egg.

7. Bake on the middle shelf of the oven for 25 minutes or until the pastry is golden brown. Serve piping hot, with mash and green veg if you like.

PEPPERONI CHICKEN TRAYBAKE

No-fuss and low-mess, this one-tray chicken dish has loads going on – with pepperoni, roasted peppers, tomatoes, olives and herbs – and gooey, melty mozzarella on top. Play around with the ingredients and make it your own.

SERVES 4

90g sliced pepperoni

4 skinless, boneless chicken breasts

2 tbsp olive oil

1 onion, finely chopped

2 garlic cloves, finely chopped

200g roasted red peppers (from a jar), finely sliced

2 x 400g tins chopped tomatoes

100ml water

1 tsp dried oregano

100g pitted Kalamata olives

A handful of basil leaves, plus extra to finish

260g mozzarella, thinly sliced

15g Parmesan, finely grated

Salt and freshly ground black pepper

1. Preheat the oven to 200°C/Fan 180°C/Gas 6. Set aside 20 pepperoni slices (to top the chicken breasts with later); chop the rest of the pepperoni slices for the sauce.

2. Place a large non-stick frying pan over a high heat. Season both sides of the chicken breasts with salt and pepper. Add the olive oil to the pan and, when it is hot, add the chicken breasts. Fry for 2 minutes on each side until well browned. Remove the chicken from the pan and set aside on a plate.

3. Add the onion to the pan and sauté for 3–4 minutes or until translucent. Add the garlic along with the rest of the chopped pepperoni. Sauté for another 2 minutes then add the roasted peppers and chopped tomatoes.

4. Pour the water into one of the empty tomato tins, swish it around to clean out the tin, then pour it into the second tin and do the same thing. Then pour this water into the pan and add the oregano. Bring to the boil, lower the heat and simmer for 5 minutes. Taste and add some salt and pepper.

5. Pour the sauce into a roasting tin, about 30 x 25cm, and add any resting juices from the chicken. Place the chicken breasts on top and scatter the olives around them. Lay a few basil leaves on each chicken breast and cover with the reserved pepperoni (5 slices per chicken breast), then the mozzarella slices. Cook on a high oven shelf for 15 minutes.

6. Take out the tin and turn the oven grill on to medium-high. Sprinkle the Parmesan over the chicken. Once the grill is hot, place the roasting tin under it and grill for 5 minutes or until the Parmesan is golden brown. Finish with some fresh basil leaves and serve a rocket salad or green veg on the side.

FOUR-CHEESE MAC 'N' CHEESE

Mac 'n' cheese was one of my favourite teas growing up –
although we didn't make it with four cheeses, just regular
grated Cheddar. This mix of cheeses – with grainy mustard,
freshly grated nutmeg and crunchy breadcrumbs – takes it
up another level.

SERVES 6–8

1 litre whole milk

2 bay leaves

500g dried macaroni

60g butter

60g plain flour

200ml single cream

1 heaped tsp wholegrain
mustard

½ nutmeg, finely grated

30g Parmesan, finely grated

125g Cheddar, grated

100g red Leicester, grated

1 mozzarella ball (125g),
torn into large chunks

Salt and freshly ground
black pepper

TOPPING

50g fresh breadcrumbs

50g Cheddar, grated

30g Parmesan, finely grated

1. Preheat the oven to 220°C/Fan 200°C/Gas 7.

2. Pour the milk into a medium saucepan, add the bay leaves
and place over a medium-low heat to warm gently.

3. Bring a large saucepan of salted water to the boil. Add
the macaroni and cook until it's a minute away from being
al dente. (You want it to still have a bit of a bite because it
will continue to cook in the oven.)

4. Meanwhile, melt the butter in a large saucepan over a
medium heat. Add the flour and cook, stirring, for 1 minute
to make a roux. Remove the bay leaves from the milk, then
gradually whisk the milk into the roux, keeping it smooth.
Continue to whisk until the sauce thickens.

5. Lower the heat and add the cream, mustard, nutmeg and
all 4 cheeses to the sauce. Stir gently until the cheeses are

completely melted. Season with salt and pepper to taste and keep the sauce warm over a very low heat.

6. When the pasta is ready, drain it well and add to the warm sauce. Mix well and tip into a roasting tray, about 33 x 23cm.

7. For the topping, sprinkle over the breadcrumbs, then the grated Cheddar and finally the Parmesan. Place on a high shelf in the oven to cook for 20 minutes or until the topping is golden and bubbling. Serve it up while it's piping hot!

STICKY SMOKED TOFU, BROCCOLI & SHIITAKE

If you're looking for big, bold flavours, this ginger-, soy- and honey-glazed tofu ticks all the boxes. Tofu has a great texture and absorbs flavours around it brilliantly, but you could also use chicken or salmon. Never throw the broccoli stalk away – it has loads of crunch and is perfect in stir-fries.

SERVES 2

300g pack smoked tofu

1 tbsp soy sauce

200g broccoli

150g shiitake mushrooms

50g cornflour

1 tbsp vegetable or sunflower oil

STIR-FRY SAUCE

2cm piece of fresh ginger, finely grated

2 garlic cloves, finely grated

2 tbsp soy sauce

1 tbsp honey

2 tbsp fresh orange juice

1 tbsp tomato purée

1 tsp sesame oil

120ml water

A pinch of white pepper

TO FINISH

2 tbsp toasted sesame seeds

Shredded spring onions

1. Cut the tofu block in half, cut each half into 2 logs and then cut each of these into 3 or 4 pieces so you have even-sized chunks. Put these into a shallow bowl and trickle over the soy sauce. Leave to marinate for a few minutes, then turn the pieces so they soak up as much soy as possible.

2. While the tofu is marinating, prepare your stir-fry sauce. Combine all the ingredients in a small bowl and mix well. Set aside.

3. Cut the broccoli into small florets and thinly slice the stalks. To prepare the shiitake, remove the stalks and halve the mushrooms. Set the veg side.

4. Put the cornflour into a shallow dish. Dip each piece of tofu into the cornflour, turning to ensure all sides are coated.

5. Place a large non-stick frying pan over a high heat. When it is hot, add the oil and then carefully add the tofu pieces. Cook them for around 5 minutes, turning as necessary, until golden brown and crisp on all sides. Remove the tofu from the pan with a slotted spoon and place it on a plate. Set aside until needed.

6. Toss the broccoli florets and stalk into the pan and cook for 2 minutes, adding a splash of water if needed. Then add the shiitake mushrooms and stir-fry sauce and cook for 1–2 minutes or until the sauce begins to thicken a little. Add the tofu back to the pan and heat through for a minute or so.

7. Serve straight away, sprinkled with sesame seeds and finished with shredded spring onion, with rice or noodles.

SALMON & DILL BURGERS

MAKE AHEAD

Chunky salmon burgers with spring onion and dill are given a crunchy lift with quick-pickled cucumber. English mustard might seem unusual with salmon, but it brings a little wasabi-like heat. You can prep the burgers the day before and keep them in the fridge.

MAKES 4

500g skinless salmon fillet, pin-boned

1 large free-range egg, beaten

4 spring onions, finely sliced

3 tbsp dill leaves, chopped

200g fresh breadcrumbs

1 tbsp olive oil

30g butter

Salt and freshly ground black pepper

PICKLED CUCUMBER

½ cucumber, thinly sliced

100ml white wine vinegar

3 tbsp caster sugar

SAUCE

6 tbsp mayonnaise

1 tsp hot English mustard

Finely grated zest and juice of ½ lemon

TO ASSEMBLE

4 burger buns, split

4 handfuls of watercress

1. Preheat the oven to 200°C/Fan 180°C/Gas 6. Line a small baking tray with baking paper.

2. Season the salmon on both sides with salt and pepper and place on the prepared tray. Bake on the middle shelf of the oven for 10 minutes. Remove and leave to cool slightly.

3. Flake the salmon into a bowl and add the egg, spring onions, chopped dill and breadcrumbs. Season the mixture liberally with salt and pepper and mix together well with your hands. Divide the mixture into 4 portions and shape each into a patty. Keep in the fridge until needed.

4. For the pickled cucumber, put the sliced cucumber into a small heatproof bowl. Heat the wine vinegar and sugar in a small pan over a medium heat until the sugar dissolves. Remove from the heat and let cool slightly, then pour over the cucumber slices and leave to pickle for 10 minutes.

5. For the sauce, mix the mayonnaise, mustard, lemon zest and juice together in a bowl and season with salt and pepper.

6. When you're ready to cook, heat the olive oil and butter in a medium non-stick frying pan. When it is hot, add the salmon patties and cook for 2–3 minutes on each side.

7. Meanwhile, lightly toast the burger buns and drain the pickled cucumber.

8. Spread both sides of the burger buns with the sauce. Place a salmon patty on each bottom burger bun and top with the pickled cucumber. Add a handful of watercress and top with the bun lids. Serve the burgers just as they are, or with chips on the side.

PORK WITH FENNEL & CHICORY

QUICK

Pork fillet sounds fancy but it's an excellent budget-friendly alternative to chicken breasts. Flavoured here with fresh sage and oregano, I've served it with a fennel, cabbage and chicory slaw topped with blue cheese and toasted walnuts – the slight bitterness of the salad goes really well with pork.

SERVES 4

2 pork tenderloins, trimmed of any sinew

1 tbsp sage leaves, finely chopped

1 tbsp oregano leaves, finely chopped

30g butter, plus an extra 20g, chilled and diced, to finish

60ml chicken stock

Salt and freshly ground black pepper

SALAD

100g fennel, finely sliced

100g white cabbage, finely shredded

2 small red chicory bulbs, leaves separated and cut in half lengthways

1 red apple, julienned

4 tbsp extra virgin olive oil

2 tbsp cider vinegar

1 tsp Dijon mustard

50g blue cheese, crumbled

20g walnuts, toasted and roughly chopped

1. Preheat the oven to 200°C/Fan 180°C/Gas 6.

2. Cut each pork tenderloin in half so you have 4 equal-sized pieces. Sprinkle them with the chopped sage and oregano, and some salt and pepper, and roll the pieces around well so they are coated on all sides with the herby seasoning.

3. Place a medium non-stick ovenproof frying pan over a high heat, then add the 30g butter. Once it's melted and foaming, place the pork pieces in the pan and cook, turning as necessary, for 6–8 minutes until golden all over. Transfer the pan to the oven for 5 minutes to finish cooking the pork.

4. Meanwhile, for the salad, put the fennel, cabbage, chicory and apple into a large bowl. Whisk the olive oil, cider vinegar and mustard together to make a smooth dressing and pour over the salad. Season with salt and pepper and toss to mix. Pile the salad onto 4 serving plates, placing it on one side.

5. Protecting your hands with oven gloves, remove the pan from the oven and transfer the pork to a warmed plate to rest for a few minutes. Place the frying pan back on the heat and deglaze with the chicken stock, stirring and scraping up any sticky bits from the base of the pan. Add the 20g butter and swirl the pan until it is melted.

6. Slice the pork thickly, arrange on the serving plates alongside the salad and spoon over the pan juices. Scatter the blue cheese and walnuts over the salad then serve.

CRAB LINGUINE

Using ingredients like fresh crab helps make quick-cook meals a bit more exciting. This is so simple: while the pasta is cooking you make the sauce using the flavoursome brown crab meat, and then stir the white crab meat through at the end.

SERVES 2

240g dried linguine

1 tbsp olive oil

20g butter

1 banana shallot, finely chopped

1 garlic clove, finely chopped

1 red chilli, deseeded and finely chopped

80g brown crab meat

1 tbsp tomato purée

100ml dry white wine

150ml single cream

Finely grated zest of 1 lemon

100g white crab meat

Salt and freshly ground black pepper

1–2 tbsp flat-leaf parsley, finely chopped, to finish

1. Bring a large saucepan of salted water to the boil. Add the linguine, stir well and cook for 10–12 minutes until *al dente* or 'just cooked'.

2. Meanwhile, put a medium sauté pan over a medium-high heat and add the olive oil and butter. When the butter is melted and foaming, add the shallot and cook for 1 minute, then add the garlic and chilli. Stir well and sauté for another minute or so.

3. Now add the brown crab meat and tomato purée and cook for another 2 minutes, stirring occasionally. Deglaze the pan with wine and let it bubble until reduced by half. Pour in the cream, bring the sauce to a simmer and let it simmer for 2–3 minutes. Taste the sauce for seasoning and add the lemon zest.

4. As soon as the pasta is cooked, use tongs to lift it from the saucepan and place it directly in the sauce. Add a good half-ladleful of the pasta cooking water too. Toss the pasta in the sauce, using the tongs, until it's completely coated. There should be some thickened sauce in the pan but most of the sauce will be soaked up by the hot pasta.

5. Stir through the white crab meat and divide the linguine between warmed pasta bowls. Sprinkle over the chopped parsley and get stuck into this creamy and luxurious pasta dish straight away!

SMOKY BEEF & BEAN PIES

These hearty beef and bean pies, flavoured with smoky lardons and smoked sweet paprika, are ideal if you've got a hungry gang to feed. Cauliflower mixed in with the potato makes the topping lighter than regular mash, but it's great with either.
Pictured overleaf

MAKES 4

2 tbsp olive oil

100g smoked bacon lardons

2 onions, diced

2 garlic cloves, finely chopped

2 tsp smoked sweet paprika

2 tbsp tomato purée

400g beef mince (12% fat)

2 tbsp plain flour

300ml beef stock

2 x 400g tins baked beans

Salt and freshly ground black pepper

TOPPING

500g Maris Piper potatoes, peeled

200g cauliflower

50g butter

80ml single cream

120g Cheddar, grated

1. Place a large non-stick saucepan over a high heat and add the olive oil. Add the lardons and sauté for 3–4 minutes until starting to brown. Toss in the onions and sauté for 5 minutes or until softened. Add the garlic and cook for 2 minutes.

2. Add the paprika and tomato purée, stir over the heat for 1–2 minutes, then add the beef mince. Cook for 5–6 minutes, breaking the meat up with a wooden spoon as it cooks.

3. Sprinkle in the flour and cook, stirring, for 2 minutes before stirring in the beef stock. Bring to a simmer and cook for 5 minutes, then tip in the baked beans. Stir then cook for another 2–3 minutes. Taste for seasoning, adding salt and pepper as needed, and remove from the heat.

4. Preheat the oven to 200°C/Fan 180°C/Gas 6.

5. For the topping, cut the potatoes into 2cm cubes and put into a saucepan. Cover with water, add salt and bring to the boil. Reduce the heat to a simmer and cook for 10 minutes.

6. Meanwhile, cut the cauliflower into florets. Add to the potatoes and cook for another 5 minutes or until both veg are tender. Drain well and then return them to the pan.

7. Mash the veg together well, using a potato masher, then stir in the butter, cream and half the cheese. Season well with salt and pepper.

8. Divide the filling between four 20cm enamel pie dishes. Spoon the mash over the filling and spread it out evenly. Sprinkle with the remaining cheese and place the pie dishes on a baking tray. (You can cover any you're not serving straight away with foil at this point and pop them in the freezer, ready to defrost and bake as needed.)

9. Place the tray on a high shelf in the oven and bake the pies for 15–20 minutes. Then turn on the oven grill and cook for a further 3–4 minutes or until the cheese topping is golden brown. Remove the pies from the oven and leave to cool slightly before tucking in!

CHEATS & TIMESAVERS

I'm all for cutting corners when it comes to making meals at home. There are some amazing pre-prepped and quick-cook ingredients available these days that can save you time in the kitchen while still delivering incredible results. Here are some of my favourite cheat's ingredients.

CURRY PASTES Although I enjoy making my own curry pastes, there are some great pre-jarred options available. From korma through tikka masala to Madras, there's something for every spice level.

CUSTARD Whether you prefer traditional or chocolate flavour, instant custard means instant dessert. I also use custard powder for the base mix in fruit tarts.

FROZEN FRUIT Keep a couple of bags of mixed berries in the freezer so you can throw together quick and easy crumbles (like the one on page 228) and other puds. Frozen fruit makes a good speedy compote, too, warmed through in a small pan.

FROZEN PEAS AND BROAD BEANS Who doesn't have a bag of frozen peas in their freezer? I love them for the bright sweetness they bring to stews, traybakes and pasta dishes, or the ready-in-minutes soup on page 14. Frozen broad beans are another great veg back-up to add to stews and casseroles, and they save you time podding the beans yourself.

FROZEN PRAWNS A fantastic standby ingredient, frozen prawns make speedy pasta dishes, stir-fries and curries feel really special.

JARRED OR TINNED ARTICHOKES Surprisingly inexpensive to buy, I use these to add extra interest to stews and traybakes. They have an earthy, slightly bitter flavour that goes particularly well with lamb. They are also good on pizzas or in calzones.

MERINGUES Good homemade meringues are absolutely beautiful but bought ones come a close second. Ideal for quick desserts with some whipped cream and fruit – try the Eton mess on page 216.

PESTO Fresh pesto tastes more vibrant than the preserved version you buy in jars, but either makes a hard-working addition to your kitchen. Pesto goes well with fish or chicken, can be mixed into a salad dressing or, of course, used as an instant pasta sauce, perhaps with some extra bits and bobs from the fridge.

POUCHES OF COOKED RICE, QUINOA AND LENTILS These are absolute winners when it comes to quick lunches and teas. Microwaveable and ready in a couple of minutes, they produce perfect fluffy rice and quinoa, and tender lentils every time. For convenience, I use them to give texture and bulk to salads, add them to stews and serve them alongside all kinds of meat, fish and veggie dishes.

READY-ROLLED PASTRY Crisp, golden pastry always makes mealtimes feel like a real treat, and ready-rolled shortcrust and puff pastry means you can make impressive sweet and savoury pies and tarts with the minimum of time and effort.

ROASTED RED PEPPERS These pack in gorgeous Mediterranean flavours without you having to do any of the hard work roasting them yourself.

STOCK A good stock is a great way to maximise flavour in soups, meaty dishes, traybakes and pies. Buy fresh vegetable, fish, chicken, lamb or beef stock, or use a good-quality stock cube.

TINS Keeping your cupboard stocked with a range of different tinned ingredients means you will always be able to cook something tasty and filling. My kitchen essentials include:

Beans All types, including borlotti, butter beans, cannellini, haricot, kidney beans… and baked beans!

Chickpeas These add bulk and texture to stews, curries and traybakes – or you can roast them for extra crunch, as in the salad on page 34.

Coconut milk For added creaminess and extra flavour in curries.

Fruit Tinned peaches, pears and pineapple are good standbys. I use them in cakes, quick tarts and desserts – and I use tinned pineapple in the quick sweet and sour sauce on page 76.

Lentils I use these for bulking up stews, salads and curries. Lentils are also a great pairing with sausages, and help meaty meals go further.

Tomatoes and passata Endlessly versatile for quick-cook meals, I use tinned tomatoes in traybakes, curries, stews, pasta sauces and quick soups. A jar of passata is a great addition to your store-cupboard too, for speedy bolognese sauces and stews.

Tuna, sardines and anchovies These are great for flavour-rich quick pasta sauces. Tinned tuna can also be used in fish cakes.

FIVE-SPICE CHICKEN WINGS

For a crowd-pleasing tea, serve these sticky five-spice, ginger and sesame wings in the middle of the table with a leafy salad or slaw, tortilla chips and/or a blue cheese dip. You'll also be pleasantly surprised that most of the ingredients for the glaze probably exist in your kitchen right now.

SERVES 4

1kg chicken wings

2 tbsp tomato ketchup

3 tbsp soy sauce

3 tbsp orange juice

2 tbsp soft light brown sugar

1 tsp Chinese five-spice powder

2 tsp sesame oil

2.5cm piece of fresh ginger, finely grated

Toasted sesame seeds, to finish

1. Put the chicken wings into a bowl, add all the rest of the ingredients except the sesame seeds, and mix well with your hands for a couple of minutes. Cover and set aside to marinate for at least 30 minutes. The longer you leave it the better though; 2–3 hours in a cool spot is perfect.

2. Preheat the oven to 200°C/Fan 180°C/Gas 6. Line a large baking tray with baking paper (to prevent the chicken wings from sticking).

3. Lay the chicken wings on the prepared tray and spoon on the marinade. Bake on the middle shelf of the oven for 20 minutes.

4. Take the tray from the oven and turn the chicken wings over. Return to the oven for 25 minutes or until they are deep brown and the marinade has turned into a sticky sauce.

5. Serve the chicken topped with a sprinkling of toasted sesame seeds and enjoy them with a leafy side salad or slaw.

PUMPKIN & SPINACH CURRY

Pumpkin and coconut milk make this mild, chunky curry extra
sweet and creamy, while spinach stirred through at the end
gives it a fresh, green vibrancy. Making your own curry paste
is easy and you'll be amazed by the intense flavours you get.

SERVES 4

4 garlic cloves, roughly
chopped

5cm piece of fresh ginger,
roughly chopped

1 long red chilli, roughly
chopped

3 tbsp vegetable or
sunflower oil

1 tsp cumin seeds

2 onions, finely diced

1 tsp ground turmeric

2 tsp ground coriander

400g tin chopped
tomatoes (or sieved
tomatoes)

250ml vegetable stock

900g–1kg peeled deseeded
pumpkin (or butternut
squash), cut into 4cm
chunks

400ml tin coconut milk

200g baby spinach leaves

Salt and freshly ground
black pepper

1. Put the garlic, ginger and chilli into a small food processor
and blitz to a rough paste. (Alternatively, you can grate the
garlic and ginger and finely chop the chilli, then mix them all
together.) Set aside.

2. Heat the oil in a large non-stick sauté pan over a high heat.
When it is hot, add the cumin seeds and stir well. Once they
begin to sizzle, add the onions to the pan and sauté over a
high heat for 4–5 minutes or until just starting to caramelise
around the edges.

3. Add the chilli-garlic-ginger paste to the pan and stir well.
Cook, stirring, for 1 minute then add the ground spices and
½ tsp salt. Stir again and lower the heat to medium, so the
spices can cook gently.

4. When you can really smell those spices, it's time to add
the tomatoes and vegetable stock. Stir well and add the
pumpkin (or squash). Increase the heat and bring to the boil,
then lower the heat to a gentle simmer. Pop a lid on the pan
and leave to cook gently for 10 minutes.

5. Remove the lid from the sauté pan and stir in the coconut
milk. Simmer, uncovered, for another 15 minutes or until the
pumpkin (or squash) is tender. Taste for seasoning and add
salt and pepper if needed.

6. When you're about to serve up the curry, stir through the
spinach. Once it is wilted, you are ready to go. Serve with
rice or warm naan bread sprinkled with chopped coriander.

CREAMY MUSHROOM SOUP

Chestnut mushrooms and thyme are a winning combination in this quick veggie soup, which has a lovely smooth texture from the potato. Fried sage is a nice addition at the end, but don't worry if it doesn't get as crispy as you'd hoped, it's more about how it tastes.

SERVES 4

2 tbsp olive oil

30g butter

2 onions, diced

3 garlic cloves, finely chopped

750g chestnut mushrooms, quartered

2 tbsp thyme leaves, chopped

1 large potato (200g) peeled and diced

1 litre vegetable stock

150ml double cream, plus an extra 4 tbsp to finish

Salt and freshly ground black pepper

TOPPING

30g butter

A handful of sage leaves

100g baby chestnut mushrooms, thickly sliced

2 garlic cloves, thinly sliced

1. Put the olive oil and butter into a large non-stick saucepan and place over a high heat. When the butter is melted and foaming, add the onions and stir well. Cook for around 5 minutes, stirring occasionally, until softened.

2. Toss in the garlic and cook for 2 minutes, then add the mushrooms and thyme. Stir well and sauté for 4–5 minutes or until the mushrooms start to brown.

3. Add the diced potato to the pan, pour in the vegetable stock and bring to the boil. Reduce the heat to a simmer and pop a lid on. Cook for about 10 minutes or until the potatoes are completely tender.

4. Now blend the soup, using a stick blender if you have one. Alternatively, let it cool a little then blitz in a jug blender until smooth. Return the soup to the pan, pour in the cream and stir well, then place back over a medium heat.

5. While the soup is heating, prepare the topping. Place a medium frying pan over a high heat and add the butter. When it is melted and foaming, add the sage leaves to the pan and fry, stirring, for about 30 seconds until they are crispy. Remove from the pan and set aside on a plate.

6. Add the sliced mushrooms and garlic to the frying pan, with a little salt and pepper. Cook for 3 minutes or until the mushrooms are golden brown, then remove from the heat.

7. Stir the soup well and season with a little salt and pepper to taste. Ladle into warmed bowls, add a drizzle of cream and top with the mushroom and garlic mix. Finish with the crispy sage leaves.

POSH FISH FINGER BUTTY

Fish fingers are a real teatime go-to, and this is a top way of making your own, using fresh fish. With a pile of rocket leaves and a big dollop of homemade tartare sauce – all packed into brioche buns – this takes a simple meal and does it really well.

MAKES 2

300g skinless cod fillet

1 tbsp dill leaves, finely chopped

Finely grated zest of 1 lemon

50g panko breadcrumbs

30g plain flour

1 large free-range egg

Vegetable or sunflower oil, to shallow-fry

Salt and freshly ground black pepper

TARTARE SAUCE

4 tbsp mayonnaise

1 hard-boiled free-range egg, finely chopped

2 cornichons, finely chopped

1 tsp Dijon mustard

1 tsp baby capers, chopped

1 tbsp flat-leaf parsley, chopped

TO ASSEMBLE

2 large brioche rolls, split

2 handfuls of rocket leaves

1. Cut the cod into 6 equal-sized fish fingers and season well with salt and pepper on both sides.

2. Set out 3 shallow bowls: mix the dill, lemon zest and breadcrumbs together in one bowl; put the flour into the second bowl and season with salt and pepper; beat the egg in the third bowl.

3. One at a time, dust the fish fingers in the seasoned flour, shake off any excess, then dip into the egg, to coat all over. Finally, dip the fish fingers into the breadcrumb mix and make sure they are fully coated. Transfer to a plate and place in the fridge until you are ready to cook them.

4. To prepare the tartare sauce, mix all the ingredients together in a small bowl. Season with salt and pepper to taste and set aside.

5. Heat a 2cm depth of oil in a medium frying pan over a high heat. When it is hot, carefully add the fish fingers to the pan and cook for 2–3 minutes on each side or until

golden and crispy. Remove the fish fingers from the pan
with a fish slice and drain on kitchen paper.

6. Lightly toast the brioche buns and spread the tartare
sauce on both cut surfaces. Place the fish fingers on the
bottom halves of the buns, top with rocket leaves and
pop the lids on to serve.

SAUSAGES & LENTILS WITH SALSA VERDE

Sausages and lentils give a real nod to proper French- and Italian-style cooking in this hearty stew. Don't worry about making the salsa verde too smooth, it can be a nice chunky salsa to add freshness.

SERVES 4

1 tbsp olive oil

8 pork sausages

100g diced pancetta

3 banana shallots, finely diced

3 celery sticks, finely diced

1 fennel bulb, diced

2 garlic cloves, finely chopped

1 tsp fennel seeds

1 tbsp tomato purée

1 tbsp plain flour

150ml dry white wine

2 x 250g pouches cooked Puy lentils

500ml chicken stock

SALSA VERDE

A handful of flat-leaf parsley leaves

A handful of basil leaves

2 tbsp tarragon leaves

2 tsp Dijon mustard

2 tsp red wine vinegar

100ml extra virgin olive oil

Salt and freshly ground black pepper

1. Heat a large non-stick casserole pan over a medium-high heat. When hot, add the olive oil, then the sausages, and cook for around 5–6 minutes, turning as necessary, until well browned on all sides. Remove the sausages from the pan and set aside on a plate.

2. Add the pancetta to the pan and sauté for 5 minutes or until it is starting to brown. Add the shallots, celery, fennel and garlic and cook for a further 3–4 minutes. Add the fennel seeds and tomato purée, stir well and cook for 2 minutes. Now stir in the flour and cook, stirring, for 2 minutes.

3. Pour in the wine, stirring and scraping the base of the pan well. Let the wine bubble away until reduced by half then add the lentils and chicken stock. Bring to the boil and then reduce the heat to a simmer. Return the sausages to the pan and cook gently for 15–20 minutes. (You can prepare the stew ahead to this point and reheat it to serve.)

4. Meanwhile, to make the salsa verde, finely chop the parsley, basil and tarragon leaves and mix together with all the other ingredients in a small bowl until evenly blended, seasoning with salt and pepper to taste.

5. Once the sausages are cooked, divide between warmed bowls and spoon on the salsa verde. I like to eat this with big slices of crunchy baguette but it would also go well with potatoes or rice, or you can just enjoy it on its own.

CHICKEN & SAFFRON ORZO

Orzo is a fantastic store-cupboard ingredient. It works a bit like rice in a chicken and pea risotto here, but this is much easier to make because you don't have to stand around stirring. Saffron has quite an intense flavour and gives the orzo its gorgeous colour, but you can leave it out if you prefer.

SERVES 4

6 skinless, boneless chicken thighs (about 500g in total)

1 tbsp olive oil

3 tbsp oregano leaves, roughly chopped

50g butter

2 banana shallots, finely diced

2 garlic cloves, finely chopped

A large pinch of saffron strands

350g orzo pasta

120ml dry white wine

1 litre chicken stock

Finely grated zest of 1 lemon

150g frozen peas

40g Parmesan, finely grated

Salt and freshly ground black pepper

1. Place the chicken thigh fillets in a shallow dish and drizzle with the olive oil. Sprinkle with half the oregano and season well with salt and pepper. Toss to coat the chicken.

2. Heat a large non-stick sauté pan over a high heat and add half the butter. Once it is melted and foaming, add the chicken thighs to the pan and cook for 2 minutes on each side or until a lovely golden-brown colour. Remove them from the pan with a slotted spoon and set aside on a plate.

3. Add the shallots and garlic to the pan, reduce the heat to medium and sauté for around 2–3 minutes until the shallots have softened up nicely. Add the saffron and orzo to the pan and stir for another 2 minutes.

4. Turn the heat back up to high and deglaze the pan with the wine, stirring well and scraping up any sticky bits from the bottom of the pan. Simmer for a few minutes or until the wine is reduced by half then pour in the chicken stock. Bring to the boil, then reduce the heat and simmer for 10 minutes.

5. Cut the chicken thighs in half and add them back to the pan. Simmer for another 5 minutes, then add the rest of the oregano, the lemon zest and frozen peas. Stir well and heat through.

6. Lastly, add the remaining butter and half of the grated Parmesan, stir well and season with salt and pepper to taste. Divide between warmed bowls, sprinkle with the remaining Parmesan and tuck in!

LEMON & OREGANO LAMB, TOMATO & BEAN SALAD

A quick marinade – like the lemon, garlic, rosemary and oregano one used for these lamb chops – is a low-effort way to add maximum flavour to simple cuts of meat and fish. The chops are pan-seared then oven-cooked and served with a cooling cannellini bean, salty feta and crunchy veg salad.

SERVES 4

8 lamb loin chops

3 tbsp extra virgin olive oil

2 garlic cloves, finely grated

Finely grated zest of 1 lemon

1 tbsp oregano leaves, chopped

1 tbsp rosemary leaves, finely chopped

Salt and freshly ground black pepper

TOMATO AND BEAN SALAD

400g tin cannellini beans, drained and rinsed

250g cherry tomatoes, halved

200g roasted red peppers (from a jar), cut into strips

4 baby cucumbers, sliced

80g feta, diced

Juice of 1 lemon

2 tbsp extra virgin olive oil

3 tbsp flat-leaf parsley, roughly chopped

1. Put the lamb chops into a shallow dish with the olive oil, garlic, lemon zest, oregano and rosemary. Add some salt and pepper and turn the chops to coat with the mixture. Leave to marinate for 20 minutes or so.

2. Preheat the oven to 200°C/Fan 180°C/Gas 6.

3. Meanwhile, for the salad, combine all the ingredients in a large bowl. Toss to mix and season with salt and pepper to taste. Set aside in the fridge until needed.

4. Place a large non-stick frying pan over a high heat. When it is hot, using tongs, carefully add the lamb chops to the pan, holding them fat side down first. You want to render some of that fat until it becomes crisp; this will only take a minute or so. Then sear the chops for 1–2 minutes on each side until golden brown.

5. Transfer the seared lamb chops to an oven tray and place on the middle shelf of the oven for 5 minutes. Remove from the oven and leave to rest for a couple of minutes while you plate the salad onto serving plates.

6. Add a couple of lamb chops to each plate, trickle over those delicious resting juices and enjoy!

CREAMY MUSHROOM TAGLIATELLE

We always have some mushrooms knocking about at home, as both Beth and I love them. They're great fillers, cheap and tasty. Porcini mushroom paste is easy to pick up from most supermarkets and adds an underlying umami intensity to this creamy pasta sauce.

SERVES 1

125g dried tagliatelle

1 tbsp olive oil

20g butter

2 garlic cloves, finely sliced

1 tbsp thyme leaves, roughly chopped (or you could use sage or rosemary)

120g chestnut mushrooms, thickly sliced

50ml white wine

1 tbsp porcini mushroom paste

100ml single cream

2–3 tbsp finely grated Parmesan

Salt and freshly ground black pepper

1. Bring a medium saucepan of salted water to the boil over a high heat. When it comes to the boil, add the tagliatelle and stir well. Cook for around 10 minutes or until the pasta is *al dente* or 'just cooked'.

2. Meanwhile, place a medium non-stick frying pan over a moderate heat. When hot, add the olive oil and butter. Once the butter is melted, add the garlic, thyme and mushrooms. Sauté until the mushrooms are lightly browned. Season with salt and pepper and then add the wine. Increase the heat and let the wine bubble until reduced by half.

3. Now stir in the mushroom paste followed by the cream. Reduce the heat to a gentle simmer and reduce until the mixture has a sauce consistency. Take the pan off the heat.

4. When the tagliatelle is cooked, using tongs, lift it out of the water and add it directly to the sauce. Place the frying pan back over a medium heat and add a little of the pasta water to loosen the sauce. Add the Parmesan and stir the tagliatelle until it's coated in the creamy sauce.

5. When you are happy with the consistency of the sauce, transfer to a warmed bowl and enjoy, while it's hot.

MISO SALMON TRAYBAKE

For this easy traybake, roasting the broccoli and asparagus with the salmon intensifies their flavour and gives them a firmer texture compared with steaming or boiling. Sugar helps the marinade caramelise as it cooks, resulting in a sweet and sticky miso glaze that's balanced by the fiery ginger.

SERVES 4

4 skinless salmon fillets (180g each)

3 tbsp miso paste

3 tbsp mirin

3 tbsp caster sugar

2 tbsp soy sauce

2.5cm piece of fresh ginger, finely grated

300g tenderstem broccoli

20 asparagus spears

1 tsp sesame oil

2 tbsp water

100g frozen peas

2 tsp toasted sesame seeds, to finish

1. Place the salmon fillets in a shallow dish. In a small bowl, mix the miso, mirin, sugar, 1 tbsp soy sauce and the ginger together well then pour over the salmon. Turn the fillets over so that all sides are well coated in the miso mix. Cover and leave to marinate in the fridge for at least 30 minutes.

2. Preheat the oven to 220°C/Fan 200°C/Gas 7.

3. Lay the tenderstem broccoli and asparagus on a baking tray, trickle over the sesame oil, remaining 1 tbsp soy sauce and the water and mix well with your hands.

4. Spread the tenderstem broccoli and asparagus spears out in a single layer on the baking tray and lay the salmon fillets on top. Place on a high shelf in the oven and bake for 10 minutes.

5. Meanwhile, put the frozen peas into a bowl, cover with boiling water and leave for a few minutes to defrost, then drain well.

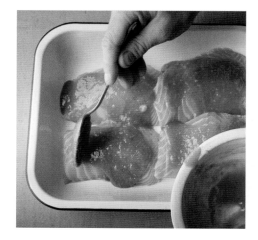

6. Take the tray from the oven and scatter the peas around the salmon fillets. Return to the oven for a couple of minutes or until the salmon and peas are cooked.

7. Take the tray from the oven and wave a cook's blowtorch over the surface of each salmon fillet to lightly caramelise the miso marinade.

8. Sprinkle the salmon with toasted sesame seeds and serve at once, with cooked rice if you like.

SWEET POTATO & KALE CURRY

I've used two types of potato in this veggie curry – sweet potatoes which work really well with the mild korma spicing, and new potatoes for their chunky texture. Kale has a bold, irony flavour and texture and I think it's amazing in curries.

SERVES 4

2 tbsp vegetable or sunflower oil

2 onions, finely diced

5 tbsp korma curry paste

500ml vegetable stock

300g sweet potatoes, peeled and cut into 4cm pieces

300g baby new potatoes

150ml single cream, plus an extra 4 tbsp to finish

2 large handfuls of kale, roughly chopped

80g roasted cashew nuts, roughly chopped

Salt and freshly ground black pepper

Coriander leaves, roughly chopped, to finish

1. Heat the oil in a large non-stick saucepan. When it's hot, add the onions and cook for 8–10 minutes or until they begin to turn a light golden brown. Stir in the korma paste and cook, stirring, for 1–2 minutes.

2. Pour in the vegetable stock and add the sweet potatoes and baby new potatoes. Bring to the boil, reduce the heat to a simmer and pop a lid on the pan. Cook until all the potatoes are tender.

3. Remove the lid, pour in the cream and toss in the chopped kale. Season with salt and pepper to taste and cook for another 3–4 minutes. Stir in half of the cashews.

4. Ladle the curry into warmed bowls and trickle over a little cream. Top with the remaining chopped cashews and finish with a scattering of chopped coriander. I like to serve this with rice flavoured with saffron, or warm naan bread.

SAUSAGE, TOMATO & BUTTER BEAN STEW

I guarantee this one-pot sausage stew will become a new regular on your midweek menu. It delivers on all fronts with filling beans, sweet cherry tomatoes and smokiness from the paprika. Get a good colour on the sausages in the pan first, as this really boosts the flavour.

SERVES 4

1 tbsp olive oil

8 pork sausages

2 onions, finely sliced

3 garlic cloves, finely chopped

1 tsp sweet smoked paprika

1 tbsp tomato purée

120ml red wine

400ml beef stock

2 tbsp rosemary leaves, roughly chopped

400g tin chopped tomatoes

2 x 400g tins butter beans, drained and rinsed

150g cherry tomatoes, halved

2 tbsp flat-leaf parsley, finely chopped

Salt and freshly ground black pepper

1. Heat a large non-stick casserole pan over a medium-high heat. When hot, add the olive oil followed by the sausages. Cook, turning, for around 5–6 minutes or until well browned on all sides. Remove them from the pan with a slotted spoon and set aside on a plate.

2. Add the onions to the pan and sauté for 2–3 minutes then add the garlic and cook for another 2 minutes. Stir in the paprika and tomato purée and cook for 1 minute before deglazing the pan with the wine. Let bubble, stirring gently, until the wine is reduced by half.

3. Add the beef stock, rosemary and tinned tomatoes and bring the sauce to the boil. Reduce the heat to a simmer and cook for 5 minutes. Now add the sausages back to the pan, along with the butter beans. Leave to simmer gently for another 5 minutes or so.

4. Lastly stir in the cherry tomatoes and cook for another 2–3 minutes or until the tomatoes are just starting to break down. Taste the sauce for seasoning and add salt and pepper as needed. Sprinkle over the chopped parsley.

5. Divide the stew between warmed bowls or plates and serve with crusty bread, or mashed potato if you prefer.

CURRIED CHICKEN TRAYBAKE

In this no-fuss family-friendly traybake, the chicken is cooked on top of the sweet potato, which gives it a nice crispy skin while the potatoes take on all that lovely chickeny flavour.

SERVES 4

400ml tin coconut milk

150ml chicken stock

2 tsp mild curry powder

2.5cm piece of fresh ginger, finely grated

2 garlic cloves, finely grated

500g sweet potato

8 chicken thighs (skin on and bone in)

200g green beans

Salt and freshly ground black pepper

1. Preheat the oven to 200°C/Fan 180°C/Gas 6.

2. Pour the coconut milk into a roasting tray, around 30 x 23cm and 6–7cm deep. Add the chicken stock, curry powder, ginger and garlic. Season well with salt and pepper and mix everything together well, using a whisk.

3. Peel the sweet potato, cut into 4cm chunks and drop these into the sauce. Season both sides of the chicken thighs with salt and pepper and lay these, skin side up, on top of the sweet potato. Try to leave the chicken skin exposed, so that it has a chance to crisp up well.

4. Place on a high shelf in the oven to cook for 30 minutes. Take the tray from the oven and add the green beans. Push them down into the sauce to ensure they will cook evenly. Return to the tray to the oven for 10–12 minutes or until the green beans are tender.

5. Divide the chicken thighs and veg between warmed plates or bowls and add a big ladleful of the curry sauce. I like to eat this with hot jasmine rice to soak up all that amazing sauce. Enjoy!

SUNDAY ROAST MEAT & VEG PASTIES

This is an amazing way of using up the leftovers from your Sunday lunch. The ratios are flexible so work with what you have – you can use beef, pork or chicken, or even just a mix of roasted veg. *Pictured overleaf*

MAKES 6

250g leftover roast meat

200g leftover veg (such as potatoes, Brussels sprouts, carrots and swede)

3 x 320g packs ready-rolled shortcrust pastry

Plain flour, to dust

100ml leftover gravy

1 large free-range egg, beaten

1. Preheat the oven to 200°C/Fan 180°C/Gas 6 and line 2 or 3 large baking trays with baking paper.

2. For the filling, cut the meat into bite-sized pieces and roughly chop the vegetables. Mix the meat and veg together and divide the filling into 6 equal portions.

3. Roll out each shortcrust pastry sheet on a lightly floured surface to a 3mm thickness. Using a plate as a guide, cut out 2 circles, about 17cm in diameter, from each sheet to give you 6 pastry circles.

4. Spoon a portion of filling onto one half of a pastry disc, leaving a clear margin around the edge. Spoon 2 tbsp of gravy onto the filling. Lightly brush the pastry margin around the filling with water, then carefully fold the other half of the pastry disc over the filling and bring the edges together so they meet. Press the edges together with your fingers to seal.

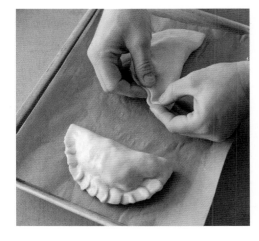

5. Crimp the pastry edges to make sure the filling is held securely inside. You can do this by pressing the pastry rim with a fork, or by making small twists along the edge and then folding the end corners underneath.

6. Repeat with the rest of the pastry circles and filling to make 6 pasties in total.

7. Carefully lift the meat and veg pasties onto the lined baking trays and brush the top of each one with beaten egg. Bake in the oven for 30–35 minutes until the pastry is crisp and golden brown.

8. Remove the pasties from the oven and leave them to cool slightly for a few minutes before eating.

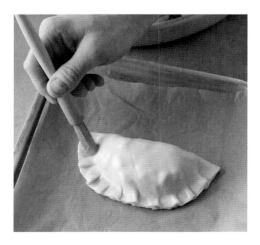

PORK CHOPS WITH CANNELLINI BEAN MASH

Pork loin steaks are perfect for quick-cook meals as they only take a few minutes in a hot pan. Mashed cannellini beans are an ideal accompaniment and make a change from regular mashed potatoes – you can also use borlotti, haricot or butter beans.

SERVES 2

2 tbsp olive oil

2 banana shallots, finely diced

2 garlic cloves, finely chopped

1 tbsp rosemary leaves, finely chopped

2 x 400g tins cannellini beans, rinsed and drained

100ml vegetable or chicken stock

100ml double cream

30g Parmesan, finely grated

Finely grated zest of 1 lemon

2 pork loin steaks (180g each)

1 tsp thyme leaves

100g cavolo nero, stalks removed

3 tbsp water

Salt and freshly ground black pepper

1. Heat 1 tbsp olive oil in a medium sauté pan over a medium heat. Add the shallots and sauté for 2–3 minutes to soften. Add the garlic and rosemary and cook, stirring, for 2 minutes then tip in the cannellini beans and pour in the stock. Cook for 3–4 minutes or until most of the stock is absorbed.

2. Now stir through the cream, grated Parmesan and lemon zest and season with salt and pepper to taste. Simmer for a couple of minutes or until the sauce is thickened. Mash the beans roughly with a potato masher and set aside.

3. Place a large non-stick frying pan over a medium heat and add the remaining olive oil. Score the fat on the pork steaks. Sprinkle the steaks on both sides with the thyme and salt and pepper.

4. Add the steaks to the pan, holding them fat side down with a pair of tongs for 1–2 minutes to render the fat until it turns golden and crispy. Then lay each pork steak down flat in the pan and cook for 2–3 minutes on each side, depending on thickness. Remove to a warm plate and leave to rest for a few minutes.

5. Meanwhile, place the pan back over a high heat and add the cavolo nero with the water. Sauté until the cavolo is tender and the water is totally reduced. Season with salt and pepper to taste.

6. Gently heat up the cannellini bean mash if necessary and divide between warmed serving plates. Place the pork steaks on the plates, spooning over any resting juices, and pile the cavolo alongside.

TOAD-IN-THE-HOLE

This is like an executive version of toad-in-the-hole, with loads of posh stuff in it – roasted tomatoes, red onion wedges, lardons – and mustard powder in the batter for extra flavour. Making the batter the day before gives a lighter, crispier result.

SERVES 4

BATTER

4 large free-range eggs

375ml whole milk

225g plain flour

1 tsp mustard powder

Salt and freshly ground black pepper

FILLING

1 tbsp olive oil

8 sausages

100g smoked bacon lardons

2 red onions, cut into wedges

200g cherry tomatoes on-the-vine

A few sprigs of thyme

1. Make the batter a day ahead, so it has time to rest. Whisk the eggs and milk together in a bowl, then whisk in the flour and mustard powder. (Don't worry if there are a few lumps, as they will break down overnight.) Cover the bowl with cling film and leave in the fridge overnight.

2. Take the batter out of the fridge an hour before you want to use it. Preheat the oven to 200°C/Fan 180°C/Gas 6.

3. Trickle the olive oil into a roasting tray, about 30 x 23cm and 6–7cm deep, and place in the oven for 10 minutes to heat up.

4. Take out the hot tray and add the sausages and lardons, then return to the oven for 8 minutes. Lift the tray out again and add the onion wedges then place back in the oven for another 5 minutes.

5. Season your batter well with salt and pepper and give it a whisk. Take the oven tray from the oven and immediately pour in the batter. Drop in the cherry tomatoes on-the-vine and thyme and put straight back into the oven on a high shelf. Bake for 35–40 minutes or until the batter is puffed up and golden brown.

6. Remove from the oven and leave your toad-in-the-hole to cool slightly before serving it up.

THREE-MUSTARD CHICKEN

I love the warmth you get from mustard – it gives a real kick but without the kind of intense heat you get from chilli. In this chicken dish, seeded mustard adds crunch, English mustard gives a real punch, and Dijon is a bit sweeter. But don't worry if you only have one type of mustard, it will still work fine.

SERVES 4

8 chicken thighs (skin on and bone in)

1 tbsp olive oil

2 banana shallots, finely sliced

4 garlic cloves, finely sliced

200ml dry white wine

400ml chicken stock

1 tbsp Dijon mustard

1 tbsp wholegrain mustard

2 tsp hot English mustard

150ml double cream

2 tbsp tarragon leaves, finely chopped

Salt and freshly ground black pepper

1. Place a large (30cm) shallow sauté pan over a low to medium heat. Season the chicken thighs on both sides with salt and pepper.

2. Add the olive oil to the pan, then add the chicken thighs, placing them skin side down. Cook, without turning, until the skin is deep golden brown and very crispy. This will take around 15 minutes (the crispy skin is worth the wait).

3. Turn the chicken thighs over and cook for 4–5 minutes on the other side. Then remove all the chicken from the pan and set it aside on a tray.

4. Increase the heat under the sauté pan to medium-high and add the shallots. Cook, stirring, for 2 minutes then add the garlic and cook for another 2 minutes. Deglaze the pan with the wine, stirring and scraping up any sticky bits from the bottom. Let the wine bubble until reduced by half, then pour in the chicken stock.

5. Now stir in all 3 mustards and the cream. Bring to the boil, reduce the heat and simmer for 5 minutes.

6. Pop the chicken back into the sauce, placing it skin side up (the skin needs to be exposed above the sauce to stay crispy). Cook for a further 8–10 minutes. Taste the sauce to check the seasoning and add some salt and pepper if you think it is needed, then sprinkle over the chopped tarragon.

7. Serve the chicken in its delicious creamy mustardy sauce with green beans and mashed potatoes on the side.

SAUSAGE & LENTIL PIES

MAKE AHEAD

Filled with sausages, lentils and veg, and topped with a creamy, fluffy potato mash and plenty of grated cheese, these pies are a complete meal in themselves. Grilling the cheese at the end makes the topping extra crispy and delicious. Be sure to use best-quality sausages.

MAKES 4

2 tbsp olive oil

8 pork sausages

1 onion, diced

2 carrots, diced

3 celery sticks, diced

2 garlic cloves, finely chopped

2 tbsp thyme leaves

1 tbsp tomato purée

2 tbsp plain flour

500ml beef stock

400g tin green lentils, drained

2 tsp Worcestershire sauce

Salt and freshly ground black pepper

MASH TOPPING

800g potatoes, peeled and cut into large chunks

100ml single cream

50ml whole milk

50g butter

75g Cheddar, grated

1. Preheat the oven to 200°C/Fan 180°C/Gas 6.

2. Heat a large non-stick casserole pan over a medium-high heat. When hot, add 1 tbsp olive oil then the sausages. Cook, turning as necessary, for around 5–6 minutes until the sausages are well browned on all sides. Remove them from the pan with a slotted spoon and set aside on a plate.

3. Heat the remaining olive oil in the pan. Add the onion and carrots, sauté for 2–3 minutes, then add the celery and garlic and cook for another 2 minutes. Stir in the thyme and tomato purée and cook for another 2 minutes.

4. Sprinkle in the flour and cook, stirring, for another minute or two. Now add the beef stock, lentils and Worcestershire sauce. Bring to the boil, then reduce the heat to a simmer and cook gently for 5 minutes.

5. For the mash topping, put the potatoes into a medium saucepan, cover with water and add some salt. Bring to the boil and cook for 10–15 minutes or until they are tender. Drain the potatoes in a colander and leave to steam off and cool slightly.

6. Meanwhile, cut each sausage into 4 or 5 pieces and add them back to the lentil mixture. Simmer for 2–3 minutes, then remove the pan from the heat. Ladle the filling into 4 individual pie dishes.

7. Put the cream, milk and butter into the empty potato pan and heat until the butter is melted. Using a potato ricer, rice the potatoes directly into the pan and mix well (or return the potatoes to the pan and mash with a potato masher) until smooth. Season with salt and pepper to taste.

8. Spoon the mash over the filling in the pie dishes, flatten with a fork to give the surface some texture and sprinkle the grated cheese evenly on top. Sit the pie dishes on a baking tray and bake on a high shelf in the oven for 15 minutes.

9. Now turn on the oven grill and cook the pies for a few more minutes until the cheese is golden brown. Take the pies out of the oven and leave them to cool slightly before tucking in.

EASY CHEESY PASTA

You can get everything you need for this comforting pasta dish from your local shop. Sliced ham and peas covered in melty cheese make it super-kid-friendly too. If you have leftover cooked sausages or veg that need eating up, chop and throw them in as well.

SERVES 2

200g pasta shells (I like to use lumaca rigata)

30g butter

150g thick sliced ham, diced

150g frozen peas (or any green veg you've got)

50ml single cream

85g Monterey Jack (or other melty cheese), grated

30g Parmesan, finely grated, plus extra (optional), to serve

Salt and freshly ground black pepper

1. Half-fill a medium saucepan with boiling water, add salt and place over a high heat. When the water is boiling, tip in the pasta shells. Stir gently as they soften and cook for around 12 minutes or until *al dente* or 'just cooked'. (The reason for the smaller amount of water than usual is so that it will have a greater concentration of starch from the pasta; this starch will help emulsify your sauce.)

2. Meanwhile, put a medium frying pan over a medium heat and add the butter. When it is melted and starting to foam, add the ham and sauté gently for a minute or so. Toss in the peas, add the cream and bring to a simmer.

3. When the pasta is cooked, remove it from the water with a slotted spoon and add it directly to the frying pan. Add a good half-ladleful of pasta water too. Add both of the grated cheeses and toss your pasta in the sauce until it starts to melt and the sauce emulsifies. Taste to check the seasoning and adjust as necessary.

4. Divide between warmed bowls and serve straight away, scattered with a little more grated Parmesan if you like.

FRIDGE RAID SOUP

This filling minestrone is the perfect way to clear out the fridge before your supermarket delivery arrives. Swap the chorizo for bacon, add beans or lentils, use only veg – anything goes. If you roughly follow these ratios of veg, chicken stock and pasta it will always taste delicious.

SERVES 4

1 tbsp olive oil

3 cooking chorizo sausages, sliced

1 large onion, diced

2 large carrots, diced

3 celery sticks, diced

2 tbsp thyme leaves

1 litre chicken stock

400g tin chopped tomatoes

150g small pasta shapes or orzo

150g frozen peas

2 large handfuls of kale, roughly chopped

Salt and freshly ground black pepper

TO FINISH

Extra virgin olive oil

Finely grated Parmesan

1. Heat the olive oil in a large saucepan. Add the chorizo slices, let them slowly render in the oil and cook for around 5 minutes or until they just begin to caramelise. Add the onion, carrots and celery and sauté for a further 5 minutes or until softened.

2. Add the thyme, chicken stock and tinned tomatoes and bring to the boil. Reduce the heat to a simmer and cook for 5 minutes before adding the pasta. Stir well and simmer for 12 minutes or until the pasta is almost cooked.

3. Toss in the frozen peas and kale, stir well and season with salt and pepper to taste. Simmer for a few minutes until the kale is tender.

4. Ladle the soup into warmed bowls. Add a drizzle of extra virgin olive oil and a sprinkling of Parmesan, then serve.

CHICKEN BURGERS

These gorgeous, crispy, golden chicken burgers taste even better than your high-street favourite. Marinating the chicken in natural yoghurt first tenderises the meat and then helps the herby, garlicky coating stick to it during cooking.

MAKES 4

4 skinless, boneless chicken thighs

200g natural yoghurt

1 tsp sweet smoked paprika

200g plain flour

1 tsp garlic powder

1 tsp dried oregano

Sunflower oil, to shallow-fry

Salt and white pepper

SAUCE

6 tbsp mayonnaise

2 tsp American mustard

1 tsp Sriracha sauce

TO ASSEMBLE

4 burger buns

12 Little Gem lettuce leaves

24 pickled cucumber burger gherkins

1. On a board, gently bash each chicken thigh fillet with a rolling pin to flatten it to an even thickness (to help it cook evenly). Place all the chicken thighs in a dish and spoon over the yoghurt, paprika and some salt and white pepper. Mix well with your hands until the chicken is well coated, then cover and leave to marinate for 30 minutes.

2. Mix the flour, garlic powder and oregano together in a shallow dish and season well with salt and white pepper; set aside. Preheat the oven to 170°C/Fan 150°C/Gas 3.

3. For the sauce, mix the ingredients together in a small bowl then set aside until ready to assemble your burgers.

4. Heat a 5cm depth of oil in a sauté pan to 170°C (check with a thermometer). Dip a chicken thigh into the flour and scrunch it into the flour on both sides, to give the coating texture; place on a tray. Repeat with the rest of the thighs.

5. To ensure a crisp coating, cook the chicken in batches. Carefully lower a couple of chicken fillets into the hot oil and

cook for 5–7 minutes, turning once. Remove with a slotted spoon and place on a wire rack over an oven tray; keep warm in the oven while you cook the remaining chicken thighs.

6. When all the chicken is done, put your burger buns into the oven for a few minutes to warm through, then split them.

7. To assemble, spread a spoonful of sauce on each bun base. Add the lettuce, then the chicken and pickles. Spread more sauce on the bun top, sandwich together and enjoy!

SARDINE, TOMATO & OLIVE PENNE

If you have a tin of sardines in your cupboard that you don't know what to do with, try this incredible punchy pasta. Using only a few ingredients, it's packed with extra flavour from olives, garlic and chilli flakes. You could also use tinned tuna.

SERVES 1

125g penne pasta

105g tin sardines in olive oil

1 shallot, finely diced

1 garlic clove, finely sliced

A pinch of dried chilli flakes

1 tsp tomato purée

125g cherry tomatoes, halved

20g pitted Kalamata olives, halved

A large handful of baby spinach leaves

Salt and freshly ground black pepper

Finely grated Parmesan, to finish (optional)

1. Bring a medium saucepan of salted water to the boil over a high heat. Add the penne and stir well. Cook for around 12 minutes or until *al dente* or 'just cooked'.

2. Meanwhile, place a non-stick frying pan over a medium heat. Open the tin of sardines and pour the oil from the tin into the frying pan (it has loads of flavour so shouldn't go to waste). Add the shallot and garlic to the pan and sauté gently for 2–3 minutes or until softened.

3. Now add the chilli flakes and tomato purée and stir with a wooden spoon over the heat for another minute, then add the cherry tomatoes and olives to the pan.

4. Give the penne a stir then take out a half-ladleful of the cooking water and add it to the frying pan; this will help create the sauce. Simmer the sauce gently for a few minutes and, as the tomatoes start to soften, press them gently with the back of your wooden spoon to release their juices.

5. When the pasta is cooked, scoop it out of the boiling water with a slotted spoon and add it straight to the frying pan, along with a little more pasta water if needed to thin the sauce.

6. Add the sardines and spinach leaves and stir again until the spinach is wilted. Taste for seasoning, adding some pepper, but go easy on the salt as the sardines and olives are both salty.

7. Serve in a warmed bowl and sprinkle on some grated Parmesan if you fancy.

CHICKEN & SPINACH CURRY

I love a good curry, and this one is quick and easy to make as it uses ready-made Madras paste, along with fresh ginger and garlic. Madras already has a good level of spice, but if you want to up the heat, throw in some chopped fresh chilli.

SERVES 4

2 tbsp vegetable or sunflower oil

2 onions, finely diced

3 garlic cloves, grated

2.5cm piece of fresh ginger, grated

5 tbsp Madras curry paste

400g tin chopped tomatoes

1kg skinless, boneless chicken thighs, cut in half

400ml coconut milk

400g new potatoes, halved

3 large handfuls of baby spinach leaves

Salt and freshly ground black pepper

Chopped coriander and sliced chilli, to finish (optional)

1. Heat the oil in a large non-stick saucepan over a high heat. When hot, add the onions and cook, stirring, for 8–10 minutes until softened and starting to turn a light golden brown. Stir in the garlic and ginger and cook for another 2 minutes.

2. Stir in the curry paste and cook, stirring, for 1–2 minutes before adding the chopped tomatoes and halved chicken thighs. Bring to a gentle simmer, pop the lid on and cook over a low heat for 10 minutes.

3. Pour in the coconut milk and add the potatoes. Increase the heat and bring to the boil, then reduce the heat to a gentle simmer. Pop the lid on and simmer gently for about 25 minutes until the chicken is cooked and the potatoes are tender. Season with salt and pepper to taste.

4. Stir in the spinach leaves and cook briefly until wilted, then remove the pan from the heat.

5. Ladle the curry into warmed bowls and finish with a scattering of chopped coriander and chilli slices if you like. Serve with rice or warm naan bread, and mango chutney if you like.

SOMETHING A BIT FANCIER

SLOW-COOKED PULLED PORK SHOULDER

Cooking pork shoulder low and slow produces succulent, tender meat that you can easily pull apart with a fork. After a bit of prep upfront to coat the pork with a smoky, sweet spice rub, sit back and let the oven do all the hard work for you.

SERVES 6

2kg boneless pork shoulder

1 tsp coarsely ground black pepper

1 tbsp sea salt

1 tbsp hot smoked paprika

1 tbsp ground cumin

2 tbsp soft light brown sugar

2 tsp garlic powder

2 tsp dried thyme

500ml dry cider (or chicken stock or beer)

100ml barbecue sauce

Hot sauce, to taste (optional)

Tortillas or soft bread rolls, to serve

1. Preheat the oven to 180°C/Fan 160°C/Gas 4.

2. Place the pork shoulder in a roasting tin in which it fits quite snugly. Mix the pepper, salt, paprika, cumin, sugar, garlic and thyme together in a small bowl. Sprinkle this spice mixture all over the pork and rub it in well on both sides. Pour the cider (or stock or beer) into the roasting tin; this will ensure everything stays moist during the lengthy cook.

3. Take a sheet of baking paper large enough to cover the tin and an equally large piece of foil; lay the foil on top of the paper. Place the layers over the roasting tin (paper side down) and tuck the edges under the rim of the tin to seal well. Cook on the middle shelf of the oven for 3–4 hours.

4. Check the meat after 3 hours to see if it is cooked and super-tender. If you press it down with the back of a spoon, the meat should collapse easily. If it's still firm, replace the paper and foil and return to the oven for a further hour.

5. Once the meat is cooked, take two forks and use them to pull it apart. Mix the pulled pork well with the pan juices. Stir through the barbecue sauce to flavour the meat, along with some hot sauce if you fancy a bit of heat. Taste and add a little more salt if needed.

6. Serve the pulled pork up in the middle of the table with some tortillas or soft bread rolls to pile the meat into. I like to add a coleslaw too, and some pickled chillies.

ROAST CHICKEN WITH ROASTED GARLIC BUTTER

Don't be alarmed by the whole bulb of garlic here. Roasting garlic softens the flavour and brings out all its sweetness. Mixed with plenty of butter, herbs and mustard, then pushed under the skin, it keeps the chicken lovely and juicy as it cooks.

SERVES 4

1 large whole garlic bulb

1 tsp extra virgin olive oil

125g butter, softened

1 tbsp thyme leaves

1 tbsp tarragon leaves, roughly chopped

1 tsp Dijon mustard

50g fresh breadcrumbs

1.8kg–2kg free-range whole chicken

1 lemon, halved

1kg new potatoes

Salt and freshly ground black pepper

1. Preheat the oven to 200°C/Fan 180°C/Gas 6.

2. Using a sharp knife, trim the top off the garlic bulb to expose the cloves. Place on a square of foil. Pour the olive oil over the garlic and season with salt and pepper. Scrunch up the foil around the garlic bulb and bake in the oven for 30 minutes or until the garlic cloves are soft when pressed. Remove from the oven and leave to cool slightly.

3. Squeeze the flesh from the garlic skins into a small bowl and mash with a fork to a smooth paste. Add the butter, herbs, mustard, breadcrumbs and some seasoning. Mix well.

4. Season the chicken all over with salt and pepper and put the lemon halves into the cavity. Gently ease the skin away from the breast of the chicken by working your fingers in between the skin and the flesh. Push the garlic butter under the skin and press down evenly. Rub any remaining butter over the chicken, including the legs and wings.

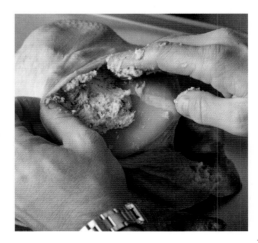

5. Place the new potatoes in a roasting dish and sit the chicken on top. Roast for 25 minutes, basting the chicken once or twice during cooking with the juices in the dish.

6. Take out the tray, lift the chicken and move the potatoes around so they cook evenly. Roast for another 30–40 minutes or until the chicken is cooked through. To test, pierce the thickest part with a skewer; the juices should run clear. Place the chicken on a warmed platter and rest for 10 minutes. Carve and serve with the roasted potatoes and green veg.

ROAST SIRLOIN WITH BABY CARROTS & SUMMER BEETS

Roast beef isn't just a great choice for a winter Sunday lunch, it makes a lovely warmer weather feast too, served with tender baby carrots and beets. Rather than a rich gravy, I've used a little of the rendered beef fat mixed with wine vinegar, mustard and chopped parsley to make a lighter dressing to pour over the top. *Pictured overleaf*

SERVES 8

1.9kg–2kg rolled sirloin of beef joint

400g baby carrots, trimmed and peeled

800g baby summer beets, peeled and halved

1–2 tbsp mild olive oil

6 sprigs of thyme

Salt and freshly ground black pepper

BEEF FAT DRESSING

4 tbsp rendered beef fat (saved from searing the meat, see method)

30ml Cabernet Sauvignon wine vinegar

1 tsp Dijon mustard

2 tbsp flat-leaf parsley, finely chopped

1. Take the beef sirloin out of the fridge at least 30 minutes before you want to start cooking. Preheat the oven to 200°C/Fan 180°C/Gas 6.

2. Remove the string from the rolled sirloin and score the fat heavily with a sharp knife – this will help the fat render when you sear the joint in the pan. Tie the rolled sirloin with new string to secure it. Season all sides of the sirloin liberally with salt and pepper.

3. Place a large heavy-based non-stick frying pan over a medium heat and lift the rolled sirloin into the pan, placing it fat side down. Sear for 15–18 minutes, turning as necessary, until the fat is well rendered and the joint of beef has a golden-brown crust all over.

4. Meanwhile, place the baby carrots and beets in a large roasting tray. Drizzle with the olive oil and scatter over the thyme sprigs. Season well with salt and pepper and toss together well.

5. Lift the sirloin out of the pan and sit it on a rack over the roasting tray of veg. Save 4 tbsp of the rendered beef fat in the frying pan for the dressing.

6. Place the roasting tray on the middle shelf of the oven and roast for 35–45 minutes or until the meat has an internal core temperature of 42–45°C (check with a digital probe thermometer).

7. Remove the roasting tray from the oven and transfer the beef joint to a warmed serving platter. Leave it to rest in a warm place for around 20 minutes (it will continue to cook as it rests).

8. Return the roasting tray to the oven to continue cooking the veg while the meat rests. (In total, the veg will cook for 55–60 minutes.)

9. Once the beef is rested, prepare the beef fat dressing. Strain the reserved beef fat into a small pan and warm through. Whisk in the wine vinegar and Dijon mustard and taste for seasoning, adding salt and pepper if needed. Stir through the chopped parsley.

10. Carve the sirloin and serve with the roasted baby carrots and summer beets, with the warm dressing spooned over.

PORK POT ROAST WITH CIDER & APPLES

This one-pot pork roast made with cider and apples is a real celebration of the West Country. Mustard adds a subtle warmth and honey lends a little sweetness. It's a stress-free way of cooking that's like a casserole, but with the meat in one piece.

SERVES 4-6

1.8kg rolled pork shoulder joint, skin scored

2 tbsp olive oil

3 onions, finely sliced

4 garlic cloves, finely sliced

3 tbsp plain flour

400ml cider

400ml chicken stock

A small bunch of thyme (tied with string)

12 sage leaves

2 bay leaves

4 Granny Smiths (or other crisp, tart eating apples)

1 tbsp wholegrain mustard

1 tsp honey

Salt and freshly ground black pepper

1. Preheat the oven to 190°C/Fan 170°C/Gas 5. Season the pork on all sides with salt and pepper, rubbing a little extra salt into the scored lines of the skin.

2. Heat the olive oil in a large non-stick casserole pan over a medium heat. Add the pork to the pan, skin side down, and colour well on all sides – the skin should be nicely crispy and browned. Lift the pork out onto a plate and set aside.

3. Add the onions to the pan and sauté for 2 minutes, then toss in the garlic and cook for another 2 minutes. Stir in the flour and cook, stirring, for another couple of minutes. Add half of the cider and chicken stock along with the herbs and stir well.

4. Bring the liquor to a gentle simmer and then return the pork to the pan. Put the lid on and place on the middle shelf of the oven to cook for 2 hours.

5. Just before the 2 hours' cooking is up, peel, quarter and core the apples. Take the pan from the oven and remove the lid. Add the apples and mustard then stir in the remaining cider and stock. Return the uncovered pan to the oven and cook for another 30 minutes.

6. Remove the pan from the oven and transfer the pork to a warmed serving platter. Leave to rest for 10 minutes before carving. Stir the honey through the sauce then taste for seasoning and adjust as necessary.

7. Carve the meat into slices and break the crackling into pieces. Serve with some apple and cider sauce and sautéed tenderstem broccoli or other green veg.

BAKED SIDE OF SALMON WITH HERB CRUST

A whole side of salmon is always an impressive way of serving fish. The herby, zesty breadcrumb crust helps keep it juicy and moist. I like my salmon quite pink inside, but you can cook it for a little longer if you prefer.

SERVES 4-6

800g side of salmon, pin-boned

3 tbsp Dijon mustard

50g panko breadcrumbs

Finely grated zest of 1 lemon

1 tbsp thyme leaves, chopped

1 tbsp flat-leaf parsley, finely chopped

1 tbsp dill leaves, finely chopped

80g butter, melted

Salt and freshly ground pepper

TO SERVE

Lemon wedges

Mayonnaise (optional)

1. Preheat the oven to 220°C/Fan 200°C/Gas 7. Line a tray (that will hold the salmon) with baking paper.

2. Lay the salmon on the tray, season well with salt and pepper and spread the mustard evenly over the surface.

3. Put the breadcrumbs, lemon zest and chopped herbs into a small bowl. Season well with salt and pepper, pour in the melted butter and mix well. Spread this crumb mixture evenly over the salmon, pressing it down gently so that it sticks well to the mustard coating.

4. Bake on a high oven shelf for 20 minutes, rotating the tray halfway through to ensure the salmon colours evenly.

5. Transfer the salmon to a warmed platter and serve with lemon wedges for squeezing and some mayonnaise too, if you fancy. Accompany with steamed new potatoes and tenderstem broccoli or green beans.

INGREDIENT SWAPS

Don't panic if you don't have everything on the ingredients list! You can usually swap a few ingredients around and still achieve a similar end result. Knowing what you can substitute will also allow you to get more creative in the kitchen and cut down on waste – you'll be able to open your fridge and cupboards and make a delicious meal with whatever you find. Below is a guide to some useful swaps and substitutions. You may need to slightly adjust your cooking times for some of them.

BEANS AND PULSES Incredibly versatile, you can usually swap these around with little impact on your final dish. Chickpeas, cannellini beans, butter beans, kidney beans, lentils and haricot beans all add bulk and protein to soups, stews, traybakes and curries. And beans make a great alternative to mashed potatoes, too – try the cannellini bean mash enriched with a little cream and lemon zest on page 132.

BRASSICAS I love the strong irony flavour and chunky texture of brassicas like kale. Most brassicas can be interchanged with similar results, including broccoli, cabbage, cauliflower, kale and kohlrabi. Don't forget to save the stalks from your broccoli too – they're great in quick stir-fries.

CHEESE Similar types of cheeses can be swapped for each other or used in combination, with very similar results.

For example, you can switch a melty Monterey Jack for Gruyère as they both behave similarly on heating. For some dishes you can use any cheese you like – most varieties would work in the four-cheese mac 'n' cheese on page 88, for example, as long as you have one good melty cheese in the mix. As a general rule though, try to stick to the same type – hard, soft, creamy, melting etc. – so you don't veer too far from the expected finish.

GREEN VEG Although some green veg have slightly different cooking times, they'll all provide a similar freshness to your mealtimes. You can happily swap any of these for each other: spinach, kale and spring greens. Asparagus and tenderstem broccoli are interchangeable, and peas, green beans and mangetout can be swapped for each other.

HERBS You can substitute most fresh herbs – or use them in combination – although they will obviously bring their own strengths, flavours and textures. Considering what each herb's texture is like will help you work out how the final dish will turn out. For example, woody herbs such as rosemary will benefit from being chopped very finely and/or are generally used in longer cooks; thyme is a suitable swap. Oregano and sage are strongly flavoured, so keep this in mind if you're introducing them into a recipe, while rosemary and thyme tend to be a bit more forgiving. Lighter leaves like mint and basil are best in salads and fresher dishes, and work in the same way as other leafy herbs like flat-leaf parsley and coriander.

MEAT, FISH AND SEAFOOD Most white fish is interchangeable – such as cod, haddock, monkfish and pollack. Oily fish like mackerel, trout and fresh sardines can also generally be swapped with each other. If a recipe calls for prawns, you can usually use thin strips of chicken or pork instead. Pork and chicken tend to work in the same way as each other in most other dishes too. Of course, you can choose any kind of sausage you like for most recipes – even merguez sausages if you like a bit of heat. When it comes to the bigger roasts, it's best to stick with the recipe as larger cuts of meat have different cooking times. Investing in a cook's thermometer to check the core temperature of a roast joint is a good way to ensure the meat is cooked through properly.

ONIONS, SHALLOTS AND LEEKS Red onions are milder and sweeter than regular brown onions, but you can use either in most recipes. Although, if a recipe calls for raw red onions – for example, in a salad or quick pickle – stick to red onions or use shallots instead. Shallots have a lovely subtle, sweet flavour, and can be used instead of regular or red onions. Leeks

have a similar flavour too, but they won't add the same level of texture. You can also use all of these in combination if you don't have enough of one type.

RICE, PASTA AND QUINOA These may be swapped with each other, and you can vary the type of rice, pasta or quinoa you use. They have different textures and cooking times but are all great for making stews and quick soups feel substantial, and for providing the carby component of most dishes, such as Beth's hide-the-veg bolognese on page 82.

ROOT VEG AND POTATOES Carrots, parsnips, swede and potatoes add bulk to a whole range of dishes, and can be substituted for each other or used in combination. Peel and chop them into similar-sized chunks for even cooking.

TINNED FRUIT Pears and peaches are easy swaps because they're both firm fruits that can withstand cooking. The spiced pear and caramel upside down cake on page 230 would be good made with tinned peaches, for example – and, likewise, for the peach and custard tarts on page 212 you could use tinned pears.

SEA BASS WITH BRAISED FENNEL & CURRIED MUSSELS

Sea bass, mussels and the mild aniseed flavour of fennel are a classic kitchen trio. Chunky sea bass fillets are simple to prep, won't dry out easily and don't taste overly fishy so they're great if you're a bit unsure about cooking fish. *Pictured overleaf*

SERVES 4

2 fennel bulbs

50g butter

150ml vegetable stock

4 sea bass fillets, skin on and pin-boned (170g each)

50g plain flour, to dust

1 tbsp olive oil

Salt and freshly ground black pepper

CURRIED MUSSELS

1kg mussels in their shells

200ml dry white wine

20g butter

2 banana shallots, finely diced

2 garlic cloves, finely chopped

2 tsp mild curry powder

150ml double cream

1. Trim the fronds from the fennel bulbs, chop them and set aside for garnish. Cut each fennel bulb into 8 wedges.

2. Place a large frying pan (one that has a lid) over a medium heat and add half the butter. Once it is melted and foaming, add the fennel wedges to the pan and sauté for 2–3 minutes on each side until light golden brown. Pour in the vegetable stock and bring to a simmer. Reduce the heat to a very low simmer and put the lid on the pan. Braise the fennel for about 10 minutes or until it is tender.

3. For the curried mussels, put a sauté pan over a high heat. Add the mussels, pour in the wine and cover with a tight-fitting lid. Shake the pan a little and let the mussels steam for about 8 minutes until all the shells have opened.

4. Drain the mussels in a fine sieve set over a bowl to catch the mussel liquor. When they are cool enough to handle, prise out the mussels and discard the shells.

5. Melt the 20g butter in the now-empty sauté pan over a medium-high heat. When the butter is starting to foam, add the shallots and garlic and cook for 3–4 minutes. Sprinkle in the curry powder and stir well for 1 minute.

6. Add the reserved mussel liquor to the sauté pan and let it bubble to reduce by half, then pour in the cream and simmer until the sauce thickens. Taste the sauce to see if it needs some seasoning (the mussel liquor may have contributed enough salt). Add the shelled mussels back to the pan to warm through.

7. Place a large non-stick frying pan over a medium-high heat. Season the sea bass fillets on both sides with salt and pepper and lightly dust all over with flour.

8. Add the olive oil to the frying pan and when it's hot, lay the sea bass fillets in the pan, skin side down. Press down on each fillet for about 5 seconds to stop the skin from curling. Leave to cook on the skin side for around 3 minutes and then flip the fillets over and add the remaining 25g butter to the pan. Cook the fish for 2 minutes on the other side.

9. Transfer the sea bass fillets to warmed plates and spoon the braised fennel alongside. Spoon the curried mussels over the sea bass and scatter over the reserved fennel fronds to serve.

BRITISH ONION SOUP

Properly caramelising the onions is the key to my British interpretation of French onion soup, which is flavoured with Bovril and Worcestershire sauce. For the cheesy sourdough toasts, get yourself a good strong Cheddar with a little acidity to counterbalance the sweetness of the onions.

SERVES 4

2 tbsp olive oil

120g unsalted butter

1kg peeled and trimmed sweet white onions (prepped weight), thinly sliced

4 garlic cloves, thinly sliced

2 tbsp thyme leaves

1 tsp soft light brown sugar

3 heaped tbsp plain flour

200ml dry white wine

1 litre good-quality beef stock

1 tsp Bovril

1–2 tbsp Worcestershire sauce, to taste

2–3 tbsp flat-leaf parsley, finely chopped

Salt and freshly ground black pepper

CHEESY TOASTS

4 slices sourdough

200g Cheddar (or your favourite British melty cheese), grated

1. Put the olive oil and butter into a large non-stick saucepan and place over a medium-high heat. When the butter is melted and foaming, add the onions. (It might seem a huge amount right now, but they will cook down a lot.) Cook the onions for around 15–20 minutes, stirring every now and then so they don't catch on the bottom of the pan.

2. Now you want to get a little colour on those onions. So, once they've started to caramelise a little, lower the heat to medium-low and let them cook really gently for another 25 minutes. Keep an eye on them and stir from time to time. They will turn a deep golden brown and turn almost jammy in consistency.

3. Next, increase the heat a little and add the garlic, thyme and brown sugar. Cook, stirring well, for 3–4 minutes then stir in the flour and cook, stirring, for a couple of minutes. Pour in the wine to deglaze the pan, stirring the onions well. Let the wine bubble away for 2 minutes before adding the beef stock. Bring to a simmer.

4. Let the soup simmer for 5 minutes then stir in the Bovril and Worcestershire sauce. Taste to check the seasoning and add some salt and pepper if needed. Keep hot.

5. Preheat the grill to medium-high and line a grill tray with foil. Toast the sourdough slices on both sides then place on the grill tray and top with the grated cheese. Place under the grill for 4–5 minutes or until the cheese is melted, golden and bubbling.

6. Ladle the onion soup into warmed bowls and sprinkle with the chopped parsley. Serve the cheesy toasts alongside for dunking.

BAKED CAMEMBERT WITH HERBY GARLIC DOUGH BALLS

This would make an amazing starter or cheese course at a dinner party. Soft, almost brioche-like dough balls are brushed with herby garlic butter and used to scoop up warm, melty Camembert. The dough is enriched with eggs, milk and butter, which makes it easy to shape.

SERVES 6–8

DOUGH BALLS

600g strong white bread flour, plus extra to dust

7g sachet fast-action dried yeast

2 tsp golden caster sugar

2 tsp salt

2 large free-range eggs, lightly beaten

180g butter, melted

200ml warm milk

A little oil, to grease

BAKED CAMEMBERT

1 Camembert (about 250g) in its wooden case

GARLIC AND HERB BUTTER

80g butter

2 garlic cloves, crushed

1 tbsp flat-leaf parsley, finely chopped

Salt and freshly ground black pepper

1. To make the dough balls, put the flour, yeast, sugar and salt into the bowl of a freestanding mixer fitted with a dough hook. Pour 2 tbsp of the beaten egg into a small bowl; set aside for later. Tip the rest of the egg into the mixer bowl, along with the melted butter and milk. Mix on a medium speed until the mixture comes together to form a dough.

2. Turn the dough out onto a very lightly floured surface and knead for 5 minutes or until it feels quite soft. Roll into a smooth ball. Clean the bowl and grease it with a little oil. Pop the dough back into the bowl and cover with a tea towel. Leave in a warm place for about an hour until the dough is doubled in size.

3. Take the Camembert out of its wooden case and set the whole cheese aside. Place the empty wooden case in the middle of a large baking tray.

4. Knead the dough to knock out the air, then divide into 24 equal pieces and roll each piece into a ball. Surround the wooden case with a ring of 10 dough balls and arrange another circle of balls around that one, spacing them a little further apart. Leave to prove in a warm place for around 30 minutes.

5. Meanwhile, preheat the oven to 200°C/Fan 180°C/Gas 6. Brush the dough balls with the reserved beaten egg and sprinkle with a little salt. Unwrap the Camembert and return it to its wooden case. Slide the baking tray onto the middle shelf of the oven and bake for 25 minutes until the dough balls are golden brown and cooked through.

6. Meanwhile, for the garlic and herb butter, melt the butter in a small saucepan over a medium heat, add the garlic and cook for 2–3 minutes. Season with salt and pepper to taste. Leave to cool slightly then stir in the chopped parsley.

7. When the dough balls are cooked, take the baking tray from the oven and spoon the garlic and herb butter over them. Serve straight away, letting everyone dip the garlicky herby dough balls into the melting Camembert.

PORK-STUFFED CABBAGE ROLLS

These little cabbage parcels are filled with minced pork, rice and pancetta, flavoured with caraway, paprika and thyme, and cooked in an easy tomato sauce. They're perfectly portioned to share around the table. You can make them the day before and keep them in the fridge overnight. *Pictured overleaf*

MAKES 18

2 large Savoy cabbages

1 tbsp olive oil

100g diced pancetta

1 large onion, finely diced

2 garlic cloves, finely diced

1 tsp caraway seeds

2 tsp paprika

1 tbsp thyme leaves

250g pouch cooked long-grain rice

400g pork mince

1 large free-range egg, lightly beaten

Salt and freshly ground black pepper

TOMATO SAUCE

1 tbsp olive oil

1 onion, finely chopped

1 tbsp tomato purée

400g tin chopped tomatoes

1 tsp dried mixed herbs

300ml chicken stock

1. Fill a large pan with boiling water and add salt. Carefully remove 18 outermost leaves from the 2 cabbages. Remove the stems from each of these leaves with a sharp knife. Add these cabbage leaves to the boiling water and cook for 2 minutes or until tender. Drain in a colander and then rinse under cold water to cool quickly; drain well.

2. Heat the olive oil in a large ovenproof sauté pan, toss in the pancetta and cook for 5 minutes until starting to brown. Add the onion and sauté for 3–4 minutes to soften. Stir in the garlic and cook for a minute, then add the caraway seeds, paprika and thyme. Stir well and then transfer the mixture to a large bowl and leave to cool completely.

3. Preheat the oven to 200°C/Fan 180°C/Gas 6. Meanwhile, make the tomato sauce. Put the sauté pan back on a medium heat and add the olive oil. When hot, add the onion and cook for 4–5 minutes or until softened. Stir in the tomato purée

and cook for 1 minute then add the chopped tomatoes, dried herbs and chicken stock. Bring the sauce to the boil, reduce the heat and simmer for 5 minutes.

4. Add the rice, pork mince and egg to the cooled pancetta mixture and season well with salt and pepper. Mix well to combine. Divide into 18 equal pieces and shape into logs.

5. Lay a cabbage leaf out flat on a work surface, place a meat log in the middle and wrap the cabbage leaf around it to seal completely. Repeat to form the rest of the cabbage rolls.

6. Carefully place the cabbage rolls in the tomato sauce in the sauté pan and cover the pan with foil. Cook on the middle shelf of the oven for 30 minutes.

7. Remove the foil and return the uncovered pan to the oven for a further 10 minutes. Serve warm from the oven.

PRAWN TACOS WITH CHILLI SALSA

If you've got some mates coming round, get some beer-battered prawn tacos on the go. Put bowls of creamy slaw and chunky chilli salsa on the table and let everyone build their own.

SERVES 4

400g large tiger prawns, halved lengthways and deveined, tails removed

Vegetable or sunflower oil, to shallow-fry

Salt and freshly ground black pepper

Lime halves, to serve

CHILLI SALSA

2 jalapeño chillies, stalks trimmed

2 shallots, peeled and halved

2 garlic cloves, peeled

2 medium tomatoes

2 tbsp extra virgin olive oil

1 tbsp coriander leaves, finely chopped

BATTER

100g plain flour

100g cornflour

1 tsp baking powder

½ tsp garlic powder

½ tsp dried oregano

½ tsp paprika

200ml cold beer

1. Preheat the oven to 240°C/Fan 220°C/Gas 9.

2. First make the chilli salsa. Lay the jalapeños, shallots, garlic and tomatoes on a small baking tray and place on the top shelf of the oven for around 8–10 minutes until the tomatoes and chillies are blistered. Remove from the oven and leave to cool slightly, then peel away the skin from the chillies and tomatoes.

3. Put the chillies and tomatoes into a small food processor, along with the shallots and garlic, and pulse briefly until you have a chunky salsa. Transfer the mixture to a small bowl and stir in the olive oil, chopped coriander and some salt and pepper; set aside.

4. To make the batter, combine all the dry ingredients in a medium bowl, and add a generous seasoning of salt and pepper. Whisk to combine and then gradually whisk in the beer to make a smooth batter. Leave to rest while you prepare the slaw.

5. To make the slaw, finely shred the cabbage and spring onions and tip into a bowl. Add the lime juice, soured cream, mayonnaise and some salt and pepper. Mix well with your hands until evenly combined. Transfer the slaw to a serving bowl and set aside.

6. You will need to cook the prawns in batches. Heat a 3–5cm depth of oil in a medium sauté pan to around 180°C. When it is hot, dip about a third of the prawns into the batter, then carefully place them in the hot oil. Cook for 1–2 minutes on each side and then remove with a slotted spoon and place on a tray lined with kitchen paper to absorb any excess oil. Repeat to cook the rest of the prawns.

SLAW

350g cabbage

4 spring onions

Juice of 1 lime

2 tbsp soured cream

2 tbsp mayonnaise

TO ASSEMBLE

16 mini flour tortillas

7. Once the prawns are all cooked, place them on a baking tray. Lay the tortillas on a couple of baking trays, too. Place the trays in the oven for 2–3 minutes to warm the tortillas and prawns through.

8. Serve the warm tortillas with the prawns, lime halves for squeezing, the chilli salsa and slaw. Let everyone dig in and help themselves.

COD WITH MUSHROOMS & CAULIFLOWER PURÉE

This pan-fried cod with cauliflower purée and wild mushrooms is based on a dish we do a lot at the Hand & Flowers. It's stylish, full of elegant flavours and on the table in less than half an hour.

SERVES 4

4 cod fillets, skin on and pin-boned (200g each)

80g butter

Juice of ½ lemon

1 tbsp extra virgin olive oil

200g wild mushrooms, halved or thickly sliced

2 tbsp flat-leaf parsley, finely chopped

Salt and freshly ground black pepper

CAULIFLOWER PURÉE

30g butter

2 banana shallots, finely diced

1 tsp mild curry powder

600g cauliflower, roughly chopped

500ml chicken stock

200ml double cream

1. First, make the cauliflower purée. Melt the butter in a medium saucepan over a medium heat. Add the shallots and sauté for 2–3 minutes or until they are softened. Stir in the curry powder and cook for 1 minute, then add the cauliflower and pour in the chicken stock. Bring to the boil, reduce the heat to a simmer and cook until the cauliflower is just tender. Then pour in the cream, increase the heat a little and let it simmer and reduce for about 10 minutes.

2. To cook the fish, place a large non-stick frying pan over a medium heat and add half the butter. Season the fish fillets on both sides with salt and pepper and lay them in the pan, skin side down. Cook for 3–4 minutes, then turn the fillets over and cook for 3–4 minutes on the other side. Remove the fish to a plate and sprinkle with lemon juice.

3. While the fish is cooking, blend the cauliflower mixture to a smooth purée, using a stick blender or jug blender. Taste and season with salt and pepper as needed. Keep warm.

4. Once you've removed the fish from the frying pan, place the pan back on the heat and add the olive oil and remaining butter. When the butter is melted and foaming, add the mushrooms with a little salt and pepper and cook over a high heat for 2–3 minutes until golden. Remove from the heat and stir through the chopped parsley.

5. Spoon the cauliflower purée into warmed bowls and place a cod fillet on each portion, then spoon on the delicious buttery mushrooms. I like eating this just as it is, but if you want to add some greens, sautéed spinach would go really well with this.

BEEF MEATBALLS WITH MARSALA & POLENTA

We usually associate meatballs with tomato sauce, but here they're cooked in a creamy Marsala sauce, a bit like a stroganoff. Marsala – a sweet fortified wine – gives the dish a rich wintry feel, especially as it's served with polenta, which makes a nice change from pasta. *Pictured overleaf*

SERVES 4

2 tbsp olive oil

1 large onion, finely chopped

2 garlic cloves, finely chopped

500g beef mince (12% fat)

1 tbsp oregano leaves, finely chopped

1 tbsp thyme leaves

50g fresh breadcrumbs

1 large free-range egg, lightly beaten

20g Parmesan, finely grated

50g plain flour, to coat

100ml Marsala

900ml beef stock

150ml double cream

1 tbsp flat-leaf parsley, finely chopped

Salt and freshly ground black pepper

1. Heat half the olive oil in a medium non-stick sauté pan. Add the onion and garlic and cook for 3–4 minutes or until the onion is softened. Take off the heat and leave to cool.

2. Put the beef mince, oregano, thyme, breadcrumbs, egg and Parmesan into a large bowl. Add the cooled onion mix and a generous seasoning of salt and pepper. Using your hands, mix everything together really well.

3. Shape the mixture into 20 equal-sized meatballs. Roll each one in flour, making sure it's coated all over, and dust off any excess flour.

4. Put the sauté pan back over a medium-high heat and add the remaining olive oil. When hot, add half the meatballs and cook, turning as necessary, for 4–5 minutes until browned all over. Using a slotted spoon, transfer them to a plate. Repeat to brown the rest of the meatballs; add to the first batch.

POLENTA

800ml chicken stock

200g quick-cook polenta

50g butter, diced

20g Parmesan, finely grated

CAVOLO

20g butter

150g cavolo nero

50ml water

5. Deglaze the pan with the Marsala, stirring and scraping up any sticky bits from the base of the pan. Let it bubble away for a minute or two, then pour the beef stock into the pan. Bring to a simmer and cook for 5 minutes. Add the cream and bring the sauce back to a gentle simmer.

6. Return all of the meatballs to the pan and simmer in the creamy sauce for 8–10 minutes or until they are cooked and the sauce is thickened. Leave over a very low heat while you prepare the sides.

7. To prepare the polenta, bring the chicken stock to a simmer in a medium saucepan over a medium-high heat, then whisk in the polenta. Stir for 1–2 minutes, or until the polenta grains swell and absorb all the liquid. Add some seasoning and stir through the butter and Parmesan.

8. To cook the cavolo, heat the butter in a large frying pan until melted and foaming. Tear the cavolo leaves in half with your hands and add them to the pan with the water and some seasoning. Stir well and cook for 3–4 minutes or until the cavolo nero is tender.

9. To serve, spoon the polenta onto warmed plates. Stir the chopped parsley through the creamy sauce and spoon the meatballs and sauce on top of the polenta. Serve the cavolo on the side.

SUMMER LAMB STEW WITH BROAD BEANS & PEAS

Vibrant with artichokes, broad beans, peas and fresh herbs, this is my light summery take on classic lamb stew. The slight bitterness of artichokes cuts through any richness in the lamb to balance the dish perfectly.

SERVES 4

800g lamb neck, cut into 2.5cm pieces

50g plain flour

3 tbsp olive oil

12 shallots, peeled and halved

3 garlic cloves, finely sliced

2 tsp thyme leaves

150ml white wine

750ml lamb or chicken stock

150g cooked artichoke hearts (tinned or chargrilled), halved

150g frozen broad beans, skinned

100g frozen peas

2 tbsp mint leaves, finely chopped

2 tbsp flat-leaf parsley, chopped

Salt and freshly ground black pepper

1. Season the lamb neck liberally on all sides with salt and pepper and then dust in the flour; shake off any excess flour.

2. Heat half the olive oil in a large non-stick casserole pan over a medium-high heat. When it is hot, add half of the lamb in a single layer and brown well for 2 minutes or so on each side. Remove from the pan and set aside on a plate. Add the rest of the oil to the pan and when it is hot, brown the remaining lamb in the same way. Remove and set aside with the rest of the meat.

3. Add the shallots to the pan and cook, stirring well, until they just begin to colour, then add the garlic and thyme leaves and stir well.

4. Pour in the wine to deglaze the pan, stirring and scraping the bottom of the pan well with a wooden spoon to release any browned bits that are stuck. Let the wine bubble away until reduced by half and then pour in the stock. Return the meat to the pan and bring the stock up to a simmer.

5. Reduce the heat to a gentle simmer and put the lid on the pan. Cook gently for 1½–2 hours, checking the stew every 20 minutes or so and giving it a gentle stir each time. When the meat is tender, the stew is ready.

6. Lastly stir through the artichokes, broad beans and peas and warm through. Just before serving, stir through the chopped mint and parsley. Serve with crusty bread on the side to mop up the delicious juices.

ROAST CHICKEN & LEEK PIE

Who doesn't get excited by a beautiful pie topped with crispy golden pastry? For the filling, chicken, leeks, lardons and peas are covered in a thick and creamy mustard sauce. Ready-rolled puff pastry makes it very easy to assemble. You can use chicken left over from a Sunday roast or shop-bought roasted chicken.

SERVES 8

70g butter

150g smoked bacon lardons

2 leeks, cut into thick rounds

100ml dry white wine

50g plain flour

250ml whole milk

250ml chicken stock

2 tbsp double cream

1½ tbsp wholegrain mustard

500g boneless roast chicken, cut into 2–3cm pieces

100g frozen peas

2 tbsp flat-leaf parsley, finely chopped

320g pack ready-rolled all-butter puff pastry

1 free-range egg, lightly beaten, to glaze

Salt and freshly ground black pepper

1. Melt 20g of the butter in a large frying pan over a medium-high heat. Add the lardons and cook for about 5 minutes until just starting to caramelise. Add the leeks and sauté for 5 minutes or until softened. Pour in the wine and let it bubble until totally reduced. Remove from the heat and set aside to cool.

2. Melt the remaining 50g butter in a large saucepan over a medium-low heat, then add the flour and cook, stirring, for 1 minute to make a roux. Swap the spoon for a whisk. Slowly add the milk and chicken stock, whisking to keep the sauce smooth. Cook, stirring, for 2–3 minutes, until thickened.

3. Remove from the heat and stir in the cream and mustard. Add the chicken and sautéed leek mixture and season with salt and pepper to taste. Transfer to a large bowl and leave to cool. Once cooled, stir in the frozen peas and parsley. (You can prepare the filling ahead to this point and keep it covered in the fridge, ready to assemble the pie and bake.)

4. Spoon the filling into a pie dish, about 28 x 18cm and 5cm deep. Roll out the pastry on a lightly floured surface until 2cm larger all round than your pie dish. Brush the rim of the dish with beaten egg. Lift the pastry over the dish and let the excess overhang. Press the edges onto the rim of the dish.

5. Brush the pastry with beaten egg and cut a small hole in the middle, to allow the steam to escape. Place in the fridge for 30 minutes to allow the pastry to rest. Meanwhile, preheat the oven to 200°C/Fan 180°C/Gas 6.

6. Bake the pie in the oven for 40 minutes or until the pastry is golden and crisp. Leave to stand for about 10 minutes before slicing and serving.

SLOW-ROASTED GARLIC & HERB LAMB SHANKS

Anchovy and garlic are beautiful with lamb so don't skip this because of the anchovies! Think of them more as a salty seasoning. Sliced potatoes and onions cook under the lamb shanks, absorbing the juices and becoming delicious and soft.

SERVES 4

4 lamb shanks

3 garlic cloves, sliced

2 tbsp rosemary leaves, roughly chopped

4 tinned anchovy fillets, finely chopped

1 tbsp extra virgin olive oil

A little softened butter, to grease the tin

1.5kg potatoes, peeled

2 onions, finely sliced

2 tbsp thyme leaves

600ml lamb or chicken stock

Salt and freshly ground black pepper

1. First, marinate the lamb shanks. Pierce each one a few times with a small sharp knife and slide a slice of garlic into each incision. Sprinkle the meat with the chopped rosemary, anchovies, olive oil and some seasoning and rub this into the meat. Leave to marinate while you prepare the potatoes.

2. Preheat the oven to 180°C/Fan 160°C/Gas 4. Lightly butter a roasting tin, about 30 x 23cm and 5cm deep.

3. Slice the potatoes very thinly using a mandoline, if you have one. Or, you can use a sharp knife; it'll just take longer.

4. Mix the sliced potatoes with the onions and thyme leaves and season generously with salt and pepper. Layer the sliced potatoes in the prepared roasting tin, overlapping them slightly. Pour in the stock then place the lamb shanks on top.

5. Take a sheet of baking paper large enough to cover the tin and an equally large piece of foil; lay the foil on top of

the paper. Place the layers over the roasting tin (paper side down) and tuck the edges under the rim of the tin to seal well. Cook on the middle shelf of the oven for 2½ hours.

6. Take out the tin and turn the oven up to 200°C/Fan 180°C/Gas 6. Remove the paper and foil cover and roast for another 25–30 minutes until the lamb shanks are well coloured.

7. Remove from the oven and leave to stand for a few minutes before serving, with a green veg of your choice.

ROAST PORK BELLY WITH FENNEL SLAW & POTATOES

I'm a huge fan of pork belly as I think it has the perfect meat to fat ratio. To get that bubbly crispy crackling, make sure the skin is really dry before you cook it. Lemony salad potatoes and a crunchy slaw complete this weekend feast.

SERVES 4–6

1.6kg boneless pork belly, skin scored

Salt and freshly ground black pepper

LEMON POTATOES

1kg Charlotte potatoes

1 tsp Dijon mustard

Juice of 1 lemon

3 tbsp extra virgin olive oil

2 tbsp finely chopped chives

FENNEL SLAW

2 fennel bulbs, trimmed

200g white cabbage, core removed

1 tsp fennel seeds, toasted and ground to a powder

2 tbsp cider vinegar

3 tbsp mayonnaise

2 tbsp dill leaves, roughly chopped

1. Take the pork out of the fridge and rub a tablespoonful of salt into the skin, making sure you get it right into the grooves of the scored skin. Leave to stand for 30 minutes. Meanwhile, preheat the oven to 170°C/Fan 150°C/Gas 3.

2. Pat the pork skin dry with kitchen paper and rub with a little more salt. Season with freshly ground pepper too. Lay the pork on a rack sitting on top of a roasting tin and roast on the middle shelf of the oven for 2 hours.

3. Meanwhile, add the potatoes to a pan of salted water, bring to the boil and cook for about 10–15 minutes until tender. Drain the potatoes, halve them when cool enough to handle and place in a bowl with the mustard, lemon juice and olive oil. Season generously with salt and pepper and toss together to combine.

4. For the fennel slaw, finely slice the fennel and tip into a large bowl. Finely shred the cabbage and add to the fennel along with the remaining ingredients. Toss together and season with salt and pepper to taste.

5. After 2 hours, take the pork out of the oven and increase the oven temperature to 240°C/Fan 220°C/Gas 9. When it reaches that heat, return the pork to the oven and roast for a further 25–30 minutes or until the skin blisters well all over and turns into crispy crackling. To ensure even cooking, rotate the pan once, halfway through. If the pork skin is not completely blistered, pop it under the grill briefly.

6. Leave the pork to rest in a warm place for 10–15 minutes before serving. Toss the potatoes with the chives. Carve the pork and serve the potatoes and fennel slaw alongside.

BARBECUE MEAT LOVERS' CALZONE

Calzones are like next-level pizzas. I love a meaty filling but feel free to mix and match your favourite ingredients – just make sure you cook any meat or veg first as it won't cook through in the calzone. *Pictured overleaf*

MAKES 4

PIZZA DOUGH

500g Italian '00' flour, plus extra to dust

½ tsp caster sugar

1 tsp salt

25g fresh yeast

325ml warm water

1 tbsp extra virgin olive oil

FILLING

200g smoked bacon lardons

1 large onion, diced

400g beef mince (12% fat)

180ml pizza sauce

4 mozzarella balls (125g each), 2 grated, 2 thinly sliced

2 jumbo frankfurters, sliced

16 slices salami

6 tbsp barbecue sauce

Olive oil, to brush

20g Parmesan, finely grated

2 tsp dried oregano

Salt and freshly ground black pepper

1. To make the pizza dough, in a large bowl, combine the flour, sugar and salt. Make a well in the middle, crumble in the fresh yeast and pour in the water and olive oil. Mix together with your hand to bring the mixture together and keep working the dough for 5 minutes or so.

2. Tip the dough out onto a floured surface and knead for another 5 minutes. Then place the dough in a clean bowl and cover with a damp cloth. Leave in a warm place until doubled in size; this will take around 15–20 minutes.

3. Preheat the oven to 240°C/Fan 220°C/Gas 9. To prepare the filling, heat a large frying pan over a high heat, then add the lardons and cook for a few minutes until the fat begins to render. Add the onion and cook for 2–3 minutes to soften.

4. Add the beef mince and cook, stirring to break up the meat, for 10–12 minutes until it is well coloured. Season with salt and pepper to taste and remove from the heat.

5. Line 2 large baking trays with baking paper. Divide the pizza dough into 4 portions. Shape each into a ball and roll out thinly on a floured surface to a round, 25cm in diameter.

6. Spread the pizza sauce over the dough rounds, leaving a 2–3cm margin. Sprinkle the grated mozzarella over one half of the sauce, dividing it equally between the 4 bases. Spoon a quarter of the beef over each cheese-topped side and cover with a quarter each of the frankfurter and salami slices. Add some barbecue sauce and top with the mozzarella slices.

7. Close the calzone by bringing the sauce-topped side over the filling so the edges meet. Fold the edges over each other to seal the parcels. Brush with a little olive oil and sprinkle with Parmesan and oregano.

8. Place the calzone on the lined trays and bake in the top of the oven for 15–20 minutes or until deep golden brown. Leave to stand for a few minutes before tucking in!

BEEF SHIN & CARROT STEW

COOKS ITSELF MAKE AHEAD

Big chunks of meat become rich and tender, and the sweetness of the carrots comes through in Acey's favourite, slow-cooked beef stew. Shin is a good choice here, as it has a great flavour and it softens beautifully in the oven.

SERVES 4–6

1kg beef shin, cut into 4cm pieces

60g plain flour

3 tbsp beef fat

2 onions, diced

3 celery sticks, diced

3 garlic cloves, finely chopped

2 tbsp tomato purée

2 tbsp thyme leaves

2 bay leaves

200ml red wine

600ml beef stock

8 medium carrots, cut into 5cm chunks

1 tsp Marmite

1 tbsp Worcestershire sauce

200g frozen peas

2 tbsp flat-leaf parsley, finely chopped

Salt and freshly ground black pepper

1. Preheat the oven to 170°C/Fan 150°C/Gas 3.

2. Season the beef liberally on all sides with salt and pepper and then dust in the flour, shaking off any excess.

3. Heat 1 tbsp beef fat in a large non-stick casserole pan over a high heat. When it is hot, add a third of the beef, in a single layer, and brown well for 2 minutes or so on each side. Remove with a slotted spoon and set aside on a plate. Add another 1 tbsp beef fat and, when hot, brown another third of the beef in the same way. Repeat to brown the final batch. Set all the meat aside.

4. Add the onions, celery and garlic to the pan and sauté for 3–4 minutes or until softened. Add the tomato purée and stir for 2 minutes, then add the thyme and bay leaves. Pour in the red wine to deglaze, stirring and scraping the base of the pan with a wooden spoon to loosen any bits that are stuck. Let the wine bubble to reduce by half, then pour in the beef stock and bring to a gentle simmer.

5. Return the browned beef to the pan and add the carrots. Bring it up to a simmer again, pop the lid on the pan and cook on the middle shelf of the oven for 2 hours. Remove the lid and return, uncovered, to the oven for a further 30 minutes or until the meat and carrots are tender.

6. Take the pan from the oven and stir through the Marmite, Worcestershire sauce, frozen peas and chopped parsley. Heat through over a medium heat on the hob then taste to check the seasoning and adjust as necessary. Serve with creamy mashed potatoes.

FISH PIE

This is a ridiculously delicious version of fish pie using smoked haddock, salmon and cod, with punchy flavours of tarragon, saffron and capers. Fish pie can sometimes be a bit bland, but these flavour spikes hitting through make it anything but dull.

SERVES 4-6

100g butter

2 leeks, halved lengthways and thickly sliced

50g plain flour

100ml dry white wine

A pinch of saffron strands

300ml fish stock

200ml whole milk

100ml crème fraîche

1 tbsp baby capers

2 tsp English mustard

100g frozen peas

2 tbsp curly parsley, finely chopped

1 tbsp tarragon leaves, finely chopped

300g skinless smoked haddock fillet, cut into 4cm chunks

300g skinless salmon fillet, cut into 4cm chunks

300g skinless cod or other white fish, cut into 4cm chunks

Salt and freshly ground black pepper

1. Preheat the oven to 200°C/Fan 180°C/Gas 6.

2. Melt half the butter in a medium frying pan over a high heat, then add the sliced leeks, sprinkle with salt and pepper and sauté for 5 minutes or until softened.

3. Remove from the heat and transfer the leeks to an ovenproof dish, about 23cm in diameter and 7–8cm deep, spreading them evenly over the bottom of the dish.

4. Melt the remaining butter in a non-stick saucepan over a medium heat. Add the flour and cook, stirring with a wooden spoon, over a medium-low heat for 2–3 minutes. Gradually stir in the wine and add the saffron. Then stir in the fish stock, followed by the milk, keeping the sauce smooth. Bring to a gentle simmer.

5. Swap the spoon for a whisk and whisk the sauce over the heat until it begins to thicken. Take the pan off the heat and stir through the crème fraîche, capers, mustard and peas. Leave the sauce to cool slightly then stir in the chopped herbs and all of the fish chunks. Spoon this mixture evenly over the leeks.

6. To prepare the mash topping, peel the potatoes, cut them into 2.5cm pieces and put into a saucepan. Cover with water, season with salt and bring to the boil. Reduce the heat to a simmer and cook for around 15 minutes, until the potatoes are tender.

7. Drain the potatoes and pass through a potato ricer if you have one, or use a potato masher to work them until smooth. Stir through the butter and crème fraîche and season well with salt and pepper.

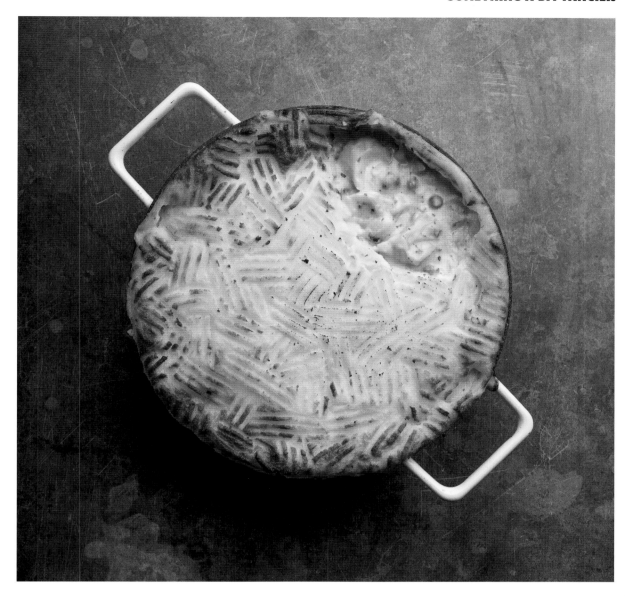

MASH TOPPING

1kg Maris Piper potatoes

50g butter

100ml crème fraîche

8. Spoon the creamy mash over the fish mixture and then use a fork to spread it evenly over the pie and create a rough textured finish. Set the dish on a baking tray and place on a high shelf in the oven. Bake for 35–40 minutes until the topping is golden.

9. Remove the fish pie from the oven and leave it to cool slightly for 5 minutes or so before serving with a green veg, such as green beans or broccoli.

MUSHROOM, SPINACH & ARTICHOKE LASAGNE

Like any lasagne, this takes a bit of work, but the end result is totally worth it. Porcini mushrooms, artichokes, fresh herbs and a whole bulb of garlic add lots of big flavour, while fresh mushrooms keep it nice and chunky, and it's super-cheesy with loads of mozzarella. The ragu, spinach and béchamel can all be made ahead, and it's a great one for freezing. *Pictured overleaf*

SERVES 6-8

30g dried porcini mushrooms

250ml boiling water

1 whole garlic bulb

3 tbsp olive oil

2 onions, finely chopped

1kg mushrooms, thickly sliced (I use a mix of portobello and chestnut)

150ml dry white wine

2 x 400g tins chopped tomatoes or cartons passata

1 tbsp thyme leaves

1 tbsp sage leaves, finely chopped

400g spinach leaves

250g fresh lasagne sheets

2 buffalo mozzarella balls (125g each), thinly sliced

250g cooked artichoke hearts (tinned or chargrilled), quartered

Salt and freshly ground black pepper

1. Preheat the oven to 200°C/Fan 180°C/Gas 6. Put the dried porcini into a heatproof bowl, pour on the boiling water and set aside to rehydrate.

2. Using a sharp knife, trim the top off the garlic bulb to expose the cloves. Place on a square of foil. Pour 1 tbsp olive oil over the garlic and season with salt and pepper. Scrunch up the foil around the garlic bulb and bake in the oven for 30 minutes or until the garlic cloves are soft when pressed. Remove from the oven and leave to cool slightly. When cool, squeeze the flesh from the garlic skins into a small bowl and mash with a fork to a smooth paste. Set aside.

3. Put the remaining 2 tbsp olive oil into a large sauté pan and place over a high heat. Add the onions and sauté for around 5 minutes until softened. Add the fresh mushrooms to the pan and cook, stirring gently, for around 5 minutes or until softened and starting to brown.

4. Deglaze the pan with the wine, stirring well, and let it bubble to reduce by half. Add the tinned tomatoes or passata to the pan with the thyme and sage. Pour a little water into one of the empty passata tins/jars, swish it around to clean out the tin, then pour that water into the second tin and do the same thing. Pour the tomato-flavoured water into the pan. Strain the porcini soaking water into the pan, too.

5. Roughly chop the porcini and add these to the pan. Bring to the boil, then reduce the heat to a simmer. Cook, stirring occasionally, for about 20 minutes. Season the mushroom ragu with salt and pepper to taste.

CHEESY BÉCHAMEL

80g butter

80g plain flour

1 litre whole milk

2 tsp Dijon mustard

1 tsp wholegrain mustard

¼ nutmeg, finely grated

50g Parmesan, finely grated

2 buffalo mozzarella balls
(125g each), diced

TOPPING

20g Parmesan, finely grated

6. Put the spinach into a large pan and add a little boiling water. Stir over a medium heat until the spinach is wilted. Drain the spinach in a colander, run some cold water over it and leave to cool. Squeeze out any excess water; set aside.

7. To make the béchamel, melt the butter in a large saucepan over a medium heat. Add the flour and cook for 1–2 minutes, stirring constantly, then gradually pour in the milk, whisking after each addition. Once all the milk is added, continue to whisk until the sauce thickens. Lower the heat and add both mustards, the nutmeg, Parmesan and diced mozzarella. Stir gently until all the cheese is fully melted. Season with salt and pepper to taste and keep it over a very low heat.

8. Spread 2–3 tbsp of mushroom ragu over the bottom of a baking dish, about 33 x 23cm and 7–8cm deep, (to stop the pasta sticking). Add a single layer of lasagne sheets and then cover with half of the ragu. Spread the spinach out over the ragu and spoon over 2–3 tbsp béchamel sauce.

9. Add another layer of lasagne sheets, then the remaining mushroom ragu. Add a layer of mozzarella slices, then the artichokes and another 2–3 tbsp of béchamel. Cover with a final layer of lasagne sheets and spread the remaining béchamel on top. Sprinkle over the extra 20g Parmesan.

10. Bake on the middle shelf of the oven for 25–30 minutes or until the lasagne sheets are tender and the cheesy top is bubbling and golden brown. Leave to stand for 5 minutes or so before serving. I like to serve this with a lightly dressed salad of mixed leaves, cucumber and cherry tomatoes.

TREATS

CHEAT'S TRIFLE

Using bought-in chocolate custard and ready-made Swiss roll, this is an easy way to knock up a super-tasty trifle. Chocolate and raspberries are always lovely together, with raspberries bringing their fresh acidity to this rich dessert.

SERVES 8

135g pack raspberry jelly

300g raspberries

80ml sherry

2 shop-bought chocolate Swiss rolls, cut into 2cm slices

500g carton Belgian chocolate custard

600ml double cream

3 tbsp icing sugar

3 tbsp Baileys (or other Irish cream liqueur)

40g dark chocolate

1. Make up the jelly according to the packet instructions and pour into a 3-litre trifle bowl. Scatter half of the raspberries evenly over the jelly and place in the fridge to set.

2. Once the jelly is set, pour the sherry into a shallow bowl. Take a couple of slices of Swiss roll, very briefly dip them into the sherry then place against the side of the trifle bowl so they stick to the glass. Repeat all around the bowl and then arrange a layer of Swiss roll slices over the jelly in the bottom of the bowl.

3. Tip the custard into the trifle bowl and spread evenly then add the remaining raspberries, in an even layer.

4. Whip the cream and icing sugar together in a bowl to soft peaks and then gently fold through the liqueur. Spoon on top of the raspberries in the trifle bowl and grate the chocolate over the surface to finish. Pop the trifle into the fridge until you are ready to serve.

BLUEBERRY BAKED CHEESECAKE

I prefer baked cheesecakes to those set with gelatine, as they have a bit more character. You're not looking for perfection here, so honestly don't worry if your cheesecake cracks on the surface in the oven, it's all part of its charm.

SERVES 9-12

BASE

250g digestive biscuits

120g butter, melted

FILLING

900g cream cheese

200g caster sugar

4 large free-range eggs, plus 1 extra egg yolk

2 tsp vanilla bean paste

Finely grated zest and juice of 1 lemon

200g crème fraîche

BLUEBERRY SAUCE

100ml water

100ml caster sugar

300g blueberries

3 tsp cornflour, mixed with 1 tbsp water

1. Preheat the oven to 180°C/Fan 160°C/Gas 4. Line the base of a 23cm round springform cake tin: flip the base of the cake tin over and lay a piece of baking paper over it, then tuck this into the open springform ring and close it over the base (so the base is flat side up); trim off excess paper.

2. Crush the digestive biscuits in a food processor (or you can pop them in a strong plastic bag and bash them gently with a rolling pin).

3. Mix the crushed biscuits with the melted butter, tip them onto the lined base of your tin and flatten down evenly with the back of a spoon. Place in the oven for 10 minutes to bake lightly, then remove and set aside to cool slightly, while you make the filling.

4. In a large bowl, beat the cream cheese to soften, using an electric whisk. Gradually beat in the sugar, whole eggs and extra egg yolk. Lastly, add the vanilla, lemon zest and juice, and the crème fraîche and beat until smoothly incorporated.

5. Pour the filling over the cheesecake base in the tin. Stand the cake tin on a baking tray and bake on a low shelf in the oven for about 45-50 minutes. Once cooked, the cheesecake should still have a slight wobble in the middle. Turn the oven off and leave the cheesecake inside to cool slowly, with the door slightly ajar.

6. Meanwhile, for the blueberry sauce, put the water and sugar into a small saucepan over a medium heat to dissolve the sugar. Bring to the boil and let boil for 2 minutes, then add the blueberries. Cook for 2–3 minutes, until the berries have released some colour into the syrup but are still plump.

Stir in the cornflour mix and cook, stirring, until the mixture thickens. Pour the blueberry sauce into a shallow dish and leave to cool. Refrigerate until you need it.

7. When ready to serve, run a palette knife around the inside of the cake tin to loosen the sides of the cheesecake, then carefully release it from the tin. Transfer the cheesecake to a serving plate and spoon the blueberry sauce over the top. Cut into wedges to serve.

PEACH & CUSTARD TARTS

MAKE AHEAD

Creamy vanilla custard sitting underneath sliced peaches makes these a bit of a mash-up between a Portuguese custard tart and a peach Danish pastry. Whatever they are, they're absolutely delicious!

MAKES 4

320g pack ready-rolled all-butter puff pastry

1 large free-range egg, beaten with a pinch of salt, to glaze

3 tbsp custard powder

2 tbsp caster sugar, plus extra to sprinkle

350ml whole milk

50ml single cream

1 tsp vanilla bean paste

410g tin peach slices in syrup, drained

2–3 tbsp flaked almonds

1. Preheat the oven to 200°C/Fan 180°C/Gas 6. Line a large baking tray with baking paper.

2. Unroll the puff pastry and cut it in half down the middle, so that you have 2 large rectangles, each about 23 x 19cm.

3. Brush one of the rectangles with beaten egg and place the other pastry rectangle on top. Gently press the pastry down and cut into 4 equal rectangles. Lay these on the lined baking tray and pop into the fridge for 15 minutes to chill.

4. Meanwhile, put the custard powder and sugar into a small pan and gradually whisk in the milk and cream. Stir in the vanilla bean paste. Place the pan over a medium-low heat and whisk until the mixture thickens. Pour the custard into a bowl and leave to cool completely.

5. Take the pastry rectangles from the fridge. Using a sharp knife, score a border 1cm in from the edge on all sides. Prick the pastry inside the border well with a fork and brush the border of each pastry rectangle with beaten egg.

6. Bake on a high shelf in the oven for 10 minutes. Remove the pastry from the oven and let cool slightly. Lightly press the middle of the rectangle down if it's risen a little.

7. Spread a quarter of the custard on each rectangle, within the border. Slice the peaches and lay on top of the custard. Scatter over the flaked almonds. Brush the pastry edges with egg and sprinkle with caster sugar. Bake on a high oven shelf for 15–20 minutes or until the pastry is golden brown. Enjoy these tarts just as they are, or with vanilla ice cream.

COFFEE CRÈME BRÛLÉE

For an easy, sophisticated dessert, try these no-bake crème brûlées. I think they're a great way to end a meal, with a few biscuits on the side. Leave out the coffee for a traditional vanilla version if you like. The brûlées can be made ahead and kept in the fridge.

MAKES 4

400ml double cream

100ml whole milk

3 tsp instant coffee granules

2 tsp vanilla bean paste

4 large free-range eggs

80g soft light brown sugar

6 tbsp caster sugar

1. Have ready four shallow ramekins or shallow heatproof bowls.

2. Combine the cream, milk, coffee and vanilla in a medium saucepan and heat gently until the coffee is dissolved.

3. Whisk the eggs and brown sugar together in a medium bowl and then gradually pour in the hot cream mixture, whisking as you do so until fully incorporated.

4. Pour the egg mixture back into the pan and place over a low heat. Cook gently, stirring constantly with a whisk or rubber spatula, until the custard is thickened. Don't let it overheat or it will curdle. Pour through a sieve into a bowl or jug and stir until it cools slightly.

5. Pour the custard evenly into the 4 ramekins or bowls and place, uncovered, in the fridge for at least 2 hours until firm to the touch. Before finishing, place the ramekins or bowls in the freezer for 10 minutes to chill the custards further.

6. When ready to serve, sprinkle 1½ tbsp caster sugar over the surface of each custard. Working with one at a time, wave a cook's blowtorch over the surface until the sugar topping melts and caramelises. (The edges will be hot so be careful when you pick them up.) Enjoy!

MIXED BERRY ETON MESS

Desserts don't get much quicker than this! Shop-bought meringues are a great cheat's tip but feel free to make your own. Raspberry syrup adds an extra layer of fruity sweetness, while Greek yoghurt brings the whole dish together to give it a fresh, summery feel.

SERVES 4

RASPBERRY SYRUP

100ml water

2 tbsp icing sugar

100g raspberries

ETON MESS

300ml whipping cream

2 tsp vanilla bean paste

2 tbsp icing sugar

200ml Greek yoghurt

125g strawberries, hulled and thickly sliced

125g blueberries

4 shop-bought meringue nests

1. To make the raspberry syrup, put the water, icing sugar and raspberries into a small saucepan over a medium heat. Mash the raspberries well, bring the mixture to the boil and cook for 2 minutes.

2. Strain the syrup through a sieve to remove the raspberry pips, then tip it back into the pan. Simmer for 3–4 minutes or until the syrup thickens slightly. Remove from the heat and leave to cool.

3. In a large bowl, whisk the cream, vanilla and icing sugar together in a bowl until firm peaks form, then fold through the yoghurt.

4. Add the strawberries and blueberries to the raspberry syrup and mix well. Add half of this mixture to the cream and yoghurt. Crumble in 3 meringues and mix well.

5. Divide this mixture between 4 serving bowls and spoon over the rest of the fruit and raspberry syrup. Roughly crumble the last meringue over the top to serve.

SELF-SAUCING CHERRY & CHOCOLATE PUDDING

Cherries and dark chocolate are such an incredible flavour combination, and this is my updated take on the classic pairing. When you bake this pudding, it produces a rich and gooey centre, so you really need to get your timings right and serve it soon after it comes out of the oven.

SERVES 6

4 tbsp cherry compote (from a jar)

200g pitted fresh cherries

175g butter, softened, plus extra to grease the dish

175g soft light brown sugar

3 large free-range eggs

1 tsp vanilla extract

175g self-raising flour

1 tsp baking powder

30g cocoa powder, plus extra to finish

A pinch of salt

80g dark chocolate, finely chopped

50ml whole milk

SAUCE

30g cocoa powder

50g soft light brown sugar

250ml boiling water

1. Preheat the oven to 180°C/Fan 160°C/Gas 4. Grease a deep 28 x 23cm baking dish well with butter.

2. Spread the cherry compote over the base of the dish, tip in the cherries and spread out evenly.

3. Using an electric whisk, beat the butter and brown sugar together in a large bowl until light and creamy. Add the eggs, one by one, whisking well after each addition. (Don't worry if the mixture begins to curdle at this point; once the flour is added it will all be ok.)

4. Add the vanilla extract, flour, baking powder, cocoa, salt, chopped chocolate and milk and continue whisking until you have a combined batter. Spoon this mixture over the cherries and spread it out evenly with the back of a spoon.

5. To make the sauce, tip the cocoa and brown sugar into a heatproof jug and mix together. Pour in the boiling water and stir well until smoothly blended.

6. Carefully pour the sauce all over the pudding mix in the dish and place on the middle shelf of the oven. Bake for 40–45 minutes or until the pudding is cooked. To check, insert a skewer into the middle; it should come out clean.

7. Remove the dish from the oven and leave the pudding to cool a little for a few minutes before serving. Dust the surface with sifted cocoa and serve with whipped cream, crème fraîche or ice cream.

STEAMED CLEMENTINE PUDDINGS

Clementines are beautiful in these individual puddings, but you can use any small oranges you like, such as mandarins or satsumas. The puddings work like mini upside-down cakes, so when you turn them out you have a perfect slice of fruit and a sticky golden syrup glaze on top.

MAKES 6

4 tbsp golden syrup

2–3 clementines

150g butter, softened, plus extra to grease the moulds

150g caster sugar

3 large free-range eggs

Finely grated zest of 1 clementine

1 tsp vanilla bean paste

150g self-raising flour

50g ground almonds

2 tbsp whole milk

CLEMENTINE SYRUP

200ml clementine juice (from about 8 clementines)

4 tbsp golden syrup

1. Preheat the oven to 180°C/Fan 160°C/Gas 4. Grease six 150ml metal dariole or pudding moulds with butter.

2. Cut a small circle of greaseproof paper to line the base of each mould. Cut 6 large, thin slices from the centre of the clementines (2 or 3 from each). Spoon a little golden syrup onto each paper disc and lay a clementine slice on top.

3. In a large bowl, beat the butter and sugar together, using an electric whisk, until smooth and creamy. Add the eggs, one at a time, beating after each addition. Add the remaining ingredients and beat until smooth. Spoon the mixture evenly into the dariole moulds. Stand them in a deep roasting tin.

4. Pour enough boiling water into the roasting tin to come halfway up the sides of the moulds. Cover the tin with a sheet of baking paper, then foil. Secure to the edges of the tin then place on the middle shelf of the oven to cook for 25 minutes.

5. Meanwhile, for the clementine syrup, heat the clementine juice and golden syrup together in a small pan, give it a stir and simmer for about 10–15 minutes until it turns syrupy.

6. Carefully remove the tray from the oven, remove the foil and baking paper and lift out the puddings. Loosen the edges with a palette knife and pop the puddings out onto warm serving plates. Spoon over some of the clementine syrup and serve with custard.

BRIOCHE MARMALADE BREAD & BUTTER PUDDING

This is like bread and butter pudding on steroids. Slices of sweet brioche are cooked with marmalade and vanilla custard, and topped with mixed peel and crunchy demerara. Brioche is quite an airy bread, so it absorbs a lot of the custard and you end up with a very indulgent dessert.

SERVES 6

80g butter, softened, plus extra to grease the dish

400g brioche loaf, cut into 12 slices

5 tbsp marmalade

4 large free-range eggs

80g golden caster sugar

200ml double cream

500ml whole milk

1 tsp vanilla extract

2 tbsp chopped mixed peel

2 tbsp demerara sugar

1. Grease a baking dish or roasting tin, around 30 x 22cm, with butter.

2. Lay the brioche slices out flat on a surface and spread each slice with butter and then marmalade. Arrange a layer of brioche, buttered side up, in the dish or tin, and then add another layer of brioche on top, slightly overlapping.

3. In a bowl, whisk the eggs, sugar, cream, milk and vanilla extract together until smooth. Pour this mixture over the brioche and leave to sit for 30 minutes.

4. Meanwhile, preheat the oven to 180°C/Fan 160°C/Gas 4 and put the kettle on.

5. Sprinkle the mixed peel and demerara sugar over the brioche and cover the dish/tin with foil. Stand it in a slightly bigger roasting tin and pour enough boiling water into the larger tin to come up halfway up the sides of the brioche tin. Bake on the middle shelf of the oven for 20 minutes.

6. Carefully take the tray from the oven and remove the foil. Place back in the oven for another 10 minutes. If you want a little more colour on the top of the pudding, place under the oven grill for a few minutes.

7. Remove from the oven and lift the baking dish/tin out of the water bath. Serve the pudding while still hot from the oven, with custard, vanilla ice cream or pouring cream.

RHUBARB & CUSTARD RICE PUDDINGS

Cooking the rice with egg yolks, sugar and cream gives these little puddings an almost custard-like consistency. The sweetness is offset by the sharp flavours of roasted rhubarb and raspberries. Grenadine adds a little flavour too, but it's really there for the intense colour it provides.

SERVES 4

120g pudding rice

1 litre whole milk

1 vanilla pod, split and seeds scraped

2 free-range egg yolks

50g caster sugar

100ml single cream

ROASTED RHUBARB

350g frozen rhubarb

2 tbsp grenadine

2 tbsp caster sugar

100g frozen raspberries

1. Put the rice, milk, vanilla seeds and scraped vanilla pod into a medium non-stick saucepan and place over a medium-high heat. When it comes to the boil, reduce the heat to a simmer and cook for 30–35 minutes or until the rice is tender, stirring every 5–10 minutes or so.

2. Meanwhile, preheat the oven to 200°C/Fan 180°C/Gas 6.

3. Put the frozen rhubarb into a shallow roasting dish, trickle over the grenadine and sprinkle with the sugar. Place on a high shelf in the oven for 10 minutes. Take the dish from the oven, scatter the frozen raspberries over the rhubarb and place back in the oven for another 5 minutes. Remove from the oven and give it a good stir; set aside until needed.

4. Whisk the egg yolks and sugar together in a medium bowl to combine, then add the cream and whisk again. Once the rice is tender, remove the pan from the heat and take out the vanilla pod. Add a heaped spoonful of the creamy rice to the whisked egg mixture and stir it in quickly, then add another couple of spoonfuls and stir those in too.

5. Pour the mixture into the rice pan and stir to mix well. Place the pan back over a low heat and cook gently, stirring occasionally, for 5 minutes.

6. Spoon the warm custardy rice pudding into 4 serving bowls. Spoon over the rhubarb topping and enjoy. This is one of my favourites – creamy, comforting and sweet, with a touch of tartness from the rhubarb to balance it perfectly!

LOTUS BISCOFF MOUSSE

Biscoff spread is such an irresistible combination of salt and sweet and crunch, once you've had a teaspoonful it's hard not to finish off the jar. This is a lovely way to incorporate it into a quick mousse, finished with a generous swirl of squirty cream.

SERVES 4

4 Lotus Biscoff biscuits

250g Lotus Biscoff spread

2 large free-range egg whites

350ml whipping cream

TO FINISH

Squirty cream

An extra 4 Lotus Biscoff biscuits

1. Crumble a biscuit into each of four 300ml serving glasses to cover the base.

2. Put the Biscoff spread into a small saucepan and heat gently until it just begins to melt. Take off the heat, stir to loosen and then leave to cool a little. (Alternatively, put the spread into a bowl and pop in the microwave for 30 seconds then give it a stir.)

3. Place the egg whites in a very clean bowl. Pour the cream into another slightly larger bowl. Using an electric whisk, whisk the egg whites until they form stiff peaks.

4. Using the same beaters (don't bother to wash them), beat the whipping cream until soft peaks form. Add the cooled Biscoff spread and beat again for 5–10 seconds.

5. Using a rubber spatula, take a large spoonful of the whipped egg whites and stir through the cream until fully incorporated. Then gently fold in the remaining egg whites, a big spoonful at a time, until fully incorporated.

6. Divide the mousse evenly between the serving glasses and pop these into the fridge for an hour or so to firm up. When ready to serve, top with squirty cream and sit another biscuit in the cream.

FRUIT CRUMBLE

Probably the best and easiest fruit crumble ever: you're just throwing a load of frozen fruit straight into a dish and topping it with apple chunks and an oaty crumble mix. Use any frozen fruit you like, except maybe banana.

SERVES 6–8

1kg frozen fruit (I often use a Black Forest mix)

2 Granny Smiths (or other crisp, tart eating apples), peeled, cored and cut into 2cm chunks

4 tbsp caster sugar

1 tsp ground mixed spice

2 tsp vanilla bean paste

Finely grated zest of 1 small lemon

CRUMBLE TOPPING

150g cold butter, diced

150g caster sugar

150g plain flour

80g rolled oats

1. Preheat the oven to 200°C/Fan 180°C/Gas 6. Have ready a deep baking dish, about 27 x 23cm.

2. Tip the frozen fruit into the dish, add the apple chunks and spread out to cover the base. Sprinkle the sugar and spice evenly over the fruit. Dot the vanilla paste over the surface and sprinkle with the lemon zest.

3. To make the crumble topping, put all the ingredients into a food processor and pulse until the mixtures resembles crumbs. (Alternatively, put the butter, sugar and flour into a bowl and rub together with your fingertips until the mix resembles crumbs and then stir in the oats.)

4. Grab handfuls of the crumble mixture, squeeze together and then crumble the mix over the fruit in the dish – make sure the crumble covers the fruit completely. Bake on a high shelf in the oven for 35–40 minutes until the crumble topping is crunchy and golden and the fruit underneath is softened and saucy.

5. Remove from the oven and leave the crumble to cool slightly before serving. I like mine with lots of cold custard, but you can serve it with hot custard if you like, or vanilla ice cream or cream.

SPICED PEAR & CARAMEL UPSIDE DOWN CAKE

A play on the classic pineapple upside down cake, this pudding always looks impressive when you turn it out. Making your own caramel isn't hard, just be sure to keep your eye on the sugar as it melts. *Pictured overleaf*

SERVES 9

2 x 415g tins pears halves in juice

CARAMEL

100g caster sugar

50g butter

50ml double cream

CAKE

175g butter, softened, plus extra to grease the tin

175g soft light brown sugar

3 large free-range eggs

1 tsp vanilla extract

175g self-raising flour

2 tsp ground mixed spice

A pinch of salt

1. Preheat the oven to 180°C/Fan 160°C/Gas 4. Line the base and sides of a 20cm square baking tin with baking paper, brushing the tin with some soft butter to help the paper to stick. If it has a removable base, seal the edges well so that the caramel doesn't spill out. Stand the tin on a baking tray.

2. To make the caramel, put the sugar into a small, deep saucepan and place over a medium-high heat. As the sugar begins to melt, swirl the pan gently to encourage it to melt evenly. When the sugar turns a dark caramel colour, remove from the heat and carefully add the butter and cream. It will bubble up fiercely, so wait for it to calm down before stirring with a wooden spoon. Place back on the heat and stir for 2 minutes until smoothly blended.

3. Drain the tinned pears and sit them on kitchen paper to dry slightly. Slice the pears into even-sized wedges and arrange in rows in the bottom of the lined baking tin. Pour the hot caramel evenly over the pears. Set aside.

4. Beat the butter and brown sugar together in a large bowl, using an electric whisk, until the mixture is light and creamy. Now add the eggs, one at a time, beating well after each addition. (Don't worry if the mixture begins to curdle at this point, once the flour is incorporated it will be fine.) Add the vanilla extract, flour, mixed spice and salt and whisk to a smooth batter.

5. Spoon the cake batter over the pears and smooth over with the back of the spoon to create an even layer. Bake on the middle shelf of the oven for 35–40 minutes. To check, insert a wooden cocktail stick into the middle; if it comes out clean, the cake is cooked. Remove from the oven and leave in the tin for 5 minutes to cool slightly.

6. Invert a serving plate over the cake and then, holding them tightly together, carefully turn both over so the cake sits on the plate. Remove the tin and paper. Cut the cake into slices and serve warm with custard or a scoop of ice cream.

REALLY USEFUL KIT

You don't need loads of fancy equipment to cook great meals, but there are some pieces of kit that will save you time in the kitchen, make cooking more enjoyable and help you to get the most from your ingredients. These are some items I wouldn't be without at home.

BAKING TINS Depending on how much baking you'll be doing, a standard 23cm round springform cake tin, a 1kg loaf tin, a 20cm square tin and a muffin tray will enable you to make most classic cakes.

BAKING TRAYS Deep-lipped baking trays prevent spills in the oven (I place pies on these in case the filling bubbles over during cooking), while flat baking trays make it easier to slide things on and off.

CASSEROLE PAN A sizeable pan that can be used on the hob and in the oven is great for pot roasts and slow-cooked stews and casseroles. Cooking in this way locks in all the flavour and goodness, and produces tender, succulent meat.

CERAMIC OVENPROOF DISH A versatile piece of kit for all kinds of savoury and sweet dishes. Get yourself one with deep sides (around 6–7cm).

COLANDER Ideal for draining pasta and veg, a colander can double up as a steamer, if you position it over a pan of boiling water with a lid on top.

COOK'S BLOWTORCH An easy way to create a caramelised, crispy or sticky charred effect. It might sound like a specialist piece of kit, but it is relatively inexpensive, and can really take your cooking up a notch. Always read the safety instructions before use.

ELECTRIC WHISK This makes light work of whisking egg whites and whipped cream, and you can also use it for creaming together cake and cookie mixtures.

FOOD PROCESSOR OR JUG BLENDER These small appliances are both useful for preparing soups, sauces and purées, and for combining ingredients together quickly – producing a nice, even consistency. A food processor also makes light work of chopping lots of veg.

GRATER A large box grater is perfect for grating cheese, of course, but I also use it for grating vegetables, such as carrots and courgettes, and for making quick veggie fritters. Use a micrograter (or the fine side of your box grater) for grating citrus zest, ginger and garlic.

KNIVES Sharp kitchen knives not only get the job done more quickly, they are also safer to use than blunt ones as they're less likely to slip when you are chopping and slicing. Be sure to sharpen them regularly, using either a special-purpose wet-stone sharpener or knife-sharpening steel.

LOOSE-BOTTOMED FLAN TIN For quiches, I use a loose-bottomed flan tin, about 25cm in diameter.

MIXING BOWLS A set of bowls is key for making cakes, puddings, batters, meatball mixes and doughs.

NON-STICK FRYING PAN A really good non-stick frying pan is a must for making omelettes. It also means you can cook meat and fish without the need for lots of oil. A frying pan that is suitable to go in the oven is a bonus.

PIE DISHES I love a pie and serving one up always looks like you've gone to a bit of effort. A large enamel pie dish, around 28 x 18cm and 5cm deep, is the size I use most. To make individual pies, I generally use 20cm oval enamel pie dishes.

ROASTING TIN A trusty roasting tin, about 30 x 23cm and 7–8cm deep, is one of the most useful pieces of kit to have. I use it for traybakes as well as weekend roasts.

SAUCEPANS WITH LIDS Have two or three in different sizes for cooking everything from pasta and potatoes to soups and sauces.

SPOONS AND SPATULAS A wooden spoon will be your loyal companion in the kitchen for all kinds of stirring and mixing. A slotted spoon is useful for transferring fried ingredients and pasta. Large metal spoons can double up as serving spoons and are good for egg mixtures. Use a spatula for mixing batters, cake mixtures and making omelettes. A ladle is helpful for dishing up pasta sauces, soups and stews, and for filling pie dishes.

THERMOMETERS A meat thermometer is a handy piece of kit to make sure meat is cooked through properly. It's also a good idea to use an oven thermometer to keep a check on the temperature of your oven.

TIN OPENER A store-cupboard stashed with plenty of tins makes one of these pretty essential!

TONGS Not essential, but these make moving meat around in a hot pan and lifting out cooked pasta easier.

BANANA & CHOCOLATE CHIP CUPCAKES

Sometimes you don't want 12 cupcakes, and this is when this small-batch recipe comes into its own. It's also a nice way of using up bananas that have been left in the fruit bowl and have gone gnarly and brown around the edges – they'll only make the cupcakes sweeter.

MAKES 6

1 ripe banana (110g)

½ tsp vanilla extract

2 tbsp soft light brown sugar

2 tbsp sunflower oil

1 large free-range egg, lightly beaten

2 tbsp cocoa powder

½ tsp baking powder

6 tbsp self-raising flour

A pinch of salt

A handful of chocolate chips (about 40g)

1. Preheat the oven to 180°C/Fan 160°C/Gas 4. Line a muffin tray with 6 cupcake/muffin cases.

2. Break the banana into pieces and place in a medium bowl. Mash well with a fork to a smooth paste, then add the vanilla extract, brown sugar and oil. Whisk using an electric whisk, until fully incorporated. Add the remaining ingredients and stir until evenly combined.

3. Spoon the mixture evenly into the cupcakes cases. Bake on the middle shelf of the oven for 12–15 minutes. To check, insert a wooden cocktail stick into the middle of one of them; if it comes out clean, the cupcake is cooked. If not, just pop them back in for a few more minutes.

4. Transfer to a wire rack to cool slightly. Enjoy these cupcakes with the kids while they are warm.

CARROT CAKE WITH ORANGE CREAM CHEESE ICING

The natural sweetness in carrots pairs brilliantly with sultanas, and because of all the carroty moisture, this cake stays fresh for longer. What makes it special is its orange cream cheese icing: the tangy citrus zest lifts the flavour and really sets it apart.

MAKES 8-10 SLICES

200g self-raising flour

150g soft light brown sugar

½ tsp baking powder

1 tsp ground cinnamon

½ tsp ground mixed spice

A pinch of salt

2 large free-range eggs

150ml sunflower oil

1 tsp vanilla extract

200g grated carrots

50g sultanas

50g pecan nuts, roughly chopped

ORANGE CREAM CHEESE ICING

50g butter, softened

150g icing sugar

Finely grated zest of 1 small orange

180g full-fat cream cheese

1. Preheat the oven to 180°C/Fan 160°C/Gas 4. Line a 1kg (or 2lb) loaf tin with baking paper.

2. Put the flour, sugar, baking powder, spices and salt into a large bowl and whisk briefly to mix, using an electric whisk. Add the eggs, oil and vanilla extract and whisk until smooth.

3. Add the grated carrots, sultanas and chopped pecans to the mixture and fold together with a rubber spatula until evenly combined.

4. Pour the mixture into the lined loaf tin, gently smooth the surface and bake on the middle shelf of the oven for 50 minutes–1 hour until firm to the touch.

5. Meanwhile, make the icing. Beat the butter, half the icing sugar and half the orange zest together in a bowl until evenly blended. Add half the cream cheese and beat to combine. Add the remaining icing sugar and cream cheese

and beat again until smoothly combined. Cover the bowl and place in the fridge until ready to assemble the cake.

6. Once cooked, take the carrot cake out of the oven and leave it to cool in the tin for 5 minutes, then remove to a wire rack. Leave to cool completely, then transfer to a plate.

7. Spread the orange cream cheese icing evenly over the top of the cake and finish with the remaining grated orange zest. Cut into slices to serve.

PARKIN

Make this and you'll have something to serve when the vicar comes round! An old-school English ginger cake, with dark sugar and a toasty spice mix, it's great with a cup of tea or strong coffee. It'll keep for a few days, getting a little softer the longer you leave it.

MAKES 12–16 SQUARES

80ml black treacle

120ml golden syrup

180g butter, plus extra to grease the tin

200g self-raising flour

100g fine oatmeal

2 tsp ground ginger

1 tsp ground mixed spice

100g soft dark brown sugar

A pinch of salt

1 large free-range egg, beaten

50ml whole milk

1. Preheat the oven to 180°C/Fan 160°C/Gas 4. Lightly grease a deep 20cm square baking tin with softened butter then line the tin with baking paper.

2. Pour the treacle, golden syrup and butter into a small saucepan and heat gently, stirring, until the butter is melted. Remove from the heat and leave to cool slightly.

3. In a large bowl, mix the flour, oatmeal, spices, sugar and salt together and make a well in the middle. Pour in the melted mixture and mix well. Add the egg and milk and mix again to combine.

4. Pour the mixture into the lined tin and place on a baking tray. Bake on the middle shelf of the oven for 40–45 minutes or until the cake is cooked and a little crunchy on top. Remove from the oven.

5. Leave the parkin to cool slightly in the tin before cutting into squares. It will keep well in an airtight container for up to a week.

COFFEE WALNUT CAKE WITH PRALINE

Coffee and walnut cake reminds me of going to school fetes. As kids, we hated it, but I now think it's lush! The praline is the posh bit – it takes a little bit of work but will make your cake a first-prize winner.

MAKES 8-10 SLICES

200g butter, softened, plus extra to grease the tin

200g soft light brown sugar

3 large free-range eggs

3 tsp instant coffee, dissolved in 2 tbsp hot water

200g self-raising flour

1 tsp baking powder

100g walnuts, toasted and chopped

WALNUT PRALINE

50g walnuts

80g caster sugar

COFFEE ICING

100g butter, softened

200g icing sugar

2 tsp instant coffee, dissolved in 1 tsp hot water

1. Preheat the oven to 180°C/Fan 160°C/Gas 4. Grease a 1kg (or 2lb) loaf tin with butter and line with baking paper.

2. Put all the cake ingredients, except the walnuts, into a large bowl and beat, using an electric whisk, until smooth. Fold in the walnuts, using a spatula or large metal spoon.

3. Spoon the cake mixture into the prepared loaf tin. Bake on the middle shelf of the oven for 40–45 minutes. To check the cake is cooked, insert a skewer into the middle; it should come out clean.

4. Meanwhile, for the praline, place the walnuts on a baking tray lined with baking paper. Tip the caster sugar into a small heavy-based saucepan and place over a high heat. Swirl the pan as the sugar melts and the sugar syrup colours to form a caramel. When the caramel reaches a deep golden-brown colour, carefully pour it over the walnuts and then leave the praline to cool and set.

5. Once the cake is cooked, take it from the oven and leave to cool in the tin for 5 minutes, then remove and place on a wire rack. Leave to cool completely, then transfer to a board.

6. To make the coffee icing, in a bowl, whisk the butter, icing sugar and coffee together until soft and creamy.

7. Spread the coffee icing over the top of the cake and swirl decoratively with a palette knife. Roughly chop the walnut praline and sprinkle on top of the cake to finish.

DOUBLE CHOCOLATE OAT COOKIES

Everyone needs a good recipe for chocolate chip cookies.
This one uses two types of chocolate – dark chocolate chips
add richness, and milk chocolate buttons bring the sweetness.
I've used oats in the mix to provide texture and to give the
cookies a bit of a flapjack feel.

MAKES 12

120g butter, softened

80g golden caster sugar

100g soft light brown sugar

1 large free-range egg

1 tsp vanilla extract

30g cocoa powder

80g rolled oats

200g plain flour

A pinch of salt

1 tsp baking powder

80g dark chocolate chips

24 large milk chocolate buttons

1. Preheat the oven to 200°C/Fan 180°C/Gas 6.

2. Using an electric whisk, beat the butter and both sugars together in a large bowl until smooth and creamy. Scrape the sides of the bowl with a rubber spatula. Add the egg and vanilla extract and beat again.

3. Add the cocoa and oats to the mixture and stir together to combine. Lastly, add the flour, salt, baking powder and chocolate chips and mix well to form a dough.

4. Divide the dough into 12 equal pieces and shape into balls. Place on a large baking tray, leaving space in between. Using the base of a ½ tsp measuring spoon, create a little hollow in the middle of each cookie by pressing it down on top of each one.

5. Bake on the middle shelf of the oven for 10 minutes, then take the tray from the oven and pop a couple of milk chocolate buttons in each hollow. Return the cookies to the oven for 4–5 minutes.

6. Transfer the cookies to a wire rack and leave to cool slightly before eating.

SULTANA SCONES

The difference between these and regular scones is the buttermilk. It has a lovely acidity and gives the scones a good flavour and light texture – so you can eat two! You can freeze them before baking if you like, then defrost a couple to pop in the oven when you fancy an afternoon treat.

MAKES 12

400g self-raising flour, plus extra to dust

80g butter, cubed

1 tsp baking powder

½ tsp salt

80g golden caster sugar

100g sultanas

250ml buttermilk

1 egg, beaten with a pinch of salt, to glaze

TO SERVE

Clotted cream or butter

Jam (of your choice)

1. Preheat the oven to 180°C/Fan 160°C/Gas 4. Line a large baking tray with baking paper.

2. Put the flour and butter into a large bowl and rub the butter into the flour with your fingertips until the mixture resembles breadcrumbs. Add the baking powder, salt, sugar and sultanas and mix well with a wooden spoon.

3. Pour in the buttermilk and mix just until a dough forms; don't over-work it. As soon as the dough starts to hold, turn it out onto a lightly floured surface and bring it together with your hands. Then gently roll the dough out to around a 2.5cm thickness.

4. Using a 6cm plain cutter, cut rounds out of the dough and place them on the prepared tray. Press the remaining dough back together, gently flatten again to a 2.5cm thickness and cut out a few more. Pop them onto the tray, along with the final scraps – these will still cook up ok (chef perks!). Leave the scones to rise on the tray for 30 minutes.

5. Brush the tops of the scones with a little beaten egg and bake on the middle shelf of the oven for 15 minutes or until they have risen even more and are a lovely golden colour on top. (Alternatively, you could freeze them to bake later.)

6. Serve the scones warm from the oven, split and topped with clotted cream or butter and your favourite jam, with a cuppa, of course!

INDEX

THANK YOU!

This is the big list of thank yous and once again there are so many people that actually make the pages come to life. Trying to grasp and understand the vision for this has been completely different from any other book – not creating a lifestyle fairy tale, but instead reflecting the everyday has been one of the most exciting challenges we could have faced.

So firstly, big thanks to everybody at Bloomsbury: Jon Croft, Rowan Yapp, Xa Shaw Stewart, Ellen Williams, Laura Brodie.

Thanks, also, to project editor Janet Illsley. And fist bumps to Laura Bayliss for putting all the words out of my mouth into letters that you can all read.

Next to the design team. It has been a real pleasure working with you guys at Superfantastic, Mark Arn and Gillian Campbell. And thanks to Jim Smith for his great work on layouts across the full book.

A huge thank you to Cristian Barnett and his assisting team: Lisa Paige-Smith, Aloha Bonser-Shaw and Sasha Burdian, for yet again making the photos look beautiful, accessible and not too terrifying! And a big thank you to Anna Wilkins for propping the food, me, Cristian and everybody up.

Massive thanks to Borra Garson for helping to structure and negotiate our way through another literary festival.

To everyone at Brand Pilot for building, structuring, pushing, designing and delivering. Absolute legends every single one of you!

To everyone in my pub and restaurant world that keeps those wheels turning. I know this has been a very difficult couple of years and I cannot thank you all enough for the dedication and commitment to, not just our businesses, but hospitality as a whole.

As always, a massive thank you to Mr Chris Mackett for being 'the rock'.

To my two brilliant PAs over the last couple of years, Alex Reilly and Emma Harrand. Thank you so much for always reminding me when I'm late!

Massive thanks obvs to everyone at home, Beth, Ace, Suze, Kerry, Inky, Zee and even Thomas Murray the builder who is so often at home or work, I might even charge him rent (*ha ha!*).

Lastly and most importantly, Nicole Herft and her team: Simone Shagham, Holly Cochrane, Sonali Shah. Nicole mate, yet again, you are just the best. Absolutely love every minute of working with you. Every time we do a book, you get it straight away, the recipes are amazing and the food looks beautiful.

If I've missed anyone, I am really sorry. Love you all xx

BLOOMSBURY ABSOLUTE

Bloomsbury Publishing Plc

50 Bedford Square, London, WC1B 3DP, UK

29 Earlsfort Terrace, Dublin 2, Ireland

BLOOMSBURY, BLOOMSBURY ABSOLUTE, the Diana logo and the
Absolute Press logo are trademarks of Bloomsbury Publishing Plc

First published in Great Britain 2022

A catalogue record for this book is available from the British Library

ISBN: HB: 978-1-4729-8164-6; eBook: 978-1-4729-8154-7

10 9 8 7 6 5 4 3 2 1

Project Editor: Janet Illsley
Cover and Typography: Superfantastic
Layout Design: Jim Smith
Photography: Cristian Barnett
Food Styling: Nicole Herft
Prop Styling: Anna Wilkins

Thanks, also, to Risdon & Risdon for supplying Tom's aprons for the shoot

Printed and bound in Germany by Mohn Media

FSC
www.fsc.org

MIX
Paper from
responsible sources
FSC® C011124

To find out more about our authors and books visit www.bloomsbury.com and sign up for our newsletters